What Great Teachers Do *Differently*

Fourteen Things That Matter Most

Todd Whitaker

EYE ON EDUCATION

EYE ON EDUCATION
6 DEPOT WAY WEST, SUITE 106
LARCHMONT, NY 10538
(914) 833–0551
(914) 833–0761 fax
www.eyeoneducation.com

Library of Congress Cataloging-in-Publication Data

Whitaker, Todd, 1959-
    What great teachers do differently : fourteen things that matter most / by Todd Whitaker.
        p. cm.
    Includes bibliographical references.
    ISBN 1-930556-69-1
    1. Teacher effectiveness. 2. Effective teaching. 3. Teacher-student relationships. I. Title.

LB1775.W44 2004
371.2'012--dc22

                                                    2003049279

20   19   18   17   16   15   14

Editorial and production services provided by
Richard H. Adin Freelance Editorial Services
52 Oakwood Blvd., Poughkeepsie, NY 12603-4112
(845-471-3566)

Other Titles by Todd Whitaker

What Great Principals Do Differently:
Fifteen Things That Matter Most
Todd Whitaker

Dealing With Difficult Teachers 2/e
Todd Whitaker

Dealing with Difficult Parents
(And with Parents in Difficult Situations)
Todd Whitaker and Douglas J. Fiore

Motivating and Inspiring Teachers:
The Educator's Guide for Building Staff Morale
Todd Whitaker, Beth Whitaker, and Dale Lumpa

Teaching Matters:
Motivating & Inspiring Yourself
Todd and Beth Whitaker

Feeling Great!
The Educator's Guide for Eating Better,
Exercising Smarter, and Feeling Your Best
Todd Whitaker and Jason Winkle

Also Available from Eye On Education

101 "Answers" For New Teachers And Their Mentors
Effective Teaching Tips for Daily Classroom Use
Annette Breaux

Real Teachers, Real Challenges, Real Solutions
25 Ways to Handle the Challenges
of the Classroom Effectively
Annette L. Breaux and Elizabeth Breaux

Coaching and Mentoring First-Year
and Student Teachers
India J. Podsen and Vicki M. Denmark

Achievement Now!
How to Assure No Child is Left Behind
Dr. Donald J. Fielder

The Call to Teacher Leadership
Sally J. Zepeda

Handbook on Teacher Portfolios
for Evaluation and Professional Development
Pamela D. Tucker, James H. Stronge,
and Christopher R. Gareis

The Principal as Instructional Leader
A Handbook for Supervisors
Sally J. Zepeda

Data Analysis for Comprehensive
Schoolwide Improvement
Victoria L. Bernhardt

Navigating Comprehensive School Change:
A Guide for the Perplexed
Thomas G. Chenoweth and Robert B. Everhart

Handbook on Teacher Evaluation:
Assessing and Improving Performance
James H. Stronge and Pamela D. Tucker

Handbook on Educational Specialist Evaluation:
Assessing and Improving Performance
James H. Stronge and Pamela D. Tucker

Staff Development:
Practices that Promote Leadership
in Learning Communities
Sally J. Zepeda

About the Author

Dr. Todd Whitaker is a Professor at Indiana State University in Terre Haute, Indiana. Prior to coming to Indiana in 1993, he taught mathematics and business at the junior high and high school levels in Missouri. Following his teaching experience he served as a middle school and high school principal for eight years. Dr. Whitaker also served as middle school coordinator in Jefferson City, Missouri.

Dr. Whitaker's work has been published in the areas of teacher leadership, instructional improvement, change, leadership effectiveness, technology, and middle level practices. His books include *Dealing With Difficult Teachers*, *Motivating & Inspiring Teachers*, *Dealing With Difficult Parents*, *Feeling Great!*, *Teaching Matters*, and *What Great Principals Do **Differently***.

Dr. Whitaker has made over 700 presentations at the state, national, and international levels. He is married to Beth, a former teacher and principal, who is an associate professor in the Elementary Education Department at Indiana State University. Beth and Todd have served as co-editors of *Contemporary Education*—an international educational journal. They are the parents of Katherine, Madeline, and Harrison.

Dedication

This book is dedicated to my favorite teachers: My three children: Katherine, Madeline, and Harrison. Watching them grow and sharing life with them has taught me more than I ever dreamed possible.

Acknowledgements

I would like to thank Celia Bohannon for her outstanding work in editing the original manuscript. Her ability to make sense of my grammar while keeping the heart of the book is a special gift.

I would also like to give a special thanks to my publisher, Mr. Robert Sickles. His support, energy, and confidence have enabled me to remain true to myself and help me share my vision with fellow educators.

And to Beth, my wife. Your continual love and support help me to be a better person than I could ever have been without you.

Table of Contents

Introduction

Any teacher can fill a bookshelf with books about education. Any teacher can study lists of guidelines, standards, principles, and theories. The best teachers and the worst teachers can ace exams in their undergraduate and graduate classes. The difference between more effective teachers and their less effective colleagues is not what they know. It is what they do.

This book is about *what great teachers do* that sets them apart. Clarifying what the best educators do, and then practicing it ourselves, can move us into their ranks.

This book is not meant to prescribe a narrow set of instructions. Instead, it frames the landscape of school from the perspective of great teachers. What do they see when they view their classrooms and the students in them? Where do they focus their attention? How do they spend their time and energy? What guides their decisions? How can we gain the same advantages?

There is no one answer; if there were, surely we'd all have it by now. Education is extremely complex, and so is classroom teaching. But we can work toward understanding what the best teachers do. We can gain insight into how effective we are as educators. Most of all, we can continue to refine our skills. All of us have this in common with the best teachers: No matter how good we are, we still want to be better.

The book flows from three different perspectives. I have participated in five research studies on the effectiveness of school principals. Each study was grounded in visits to more effective schools and to less effective schools. In every school, no matter what the environment, I found a wide range of teachers—some more effective, some less so. Better schools may have a higher percentage of better teachers, but I found great teachers in every setting, and I grew curious about what made them great. Second, every year I work with more than 50 schools as a consultant. Through years of observing and visiting with teachers, principals, students, and staff, I have gained insight into the attitudes and behaviors that lead to success. The third perspective is very personal: I write from my own experience as a teacher and principal. I have worked with many outstanding colleagues. What made them great? What kept others from reaching that level?

Over the years, I have presented some of my answers to these questions in sessions with school principals and other educators. And, I compiled my thoughts in a short book, *What Great Principals Do Differently*. Before long, it became evident that great principals and great teachers share many of the same qualities. It makes sense: Part of being a great principal is to be a great teacher; part of being a great teacher is to be a great leader. Educators began inviting me to their schools and districts to work with their teachers, and teachers began asking me to write a companion volume that accounts for the differences between a principal's role and a teacher's role. With my compliments to all the great teachers in our schools, here is that book.

Not all aspects of great teaching have a place in these pages. Those who seek guidance on curriculum development, instructional approaches, assessment rubrics, and other such tools of the trade will find that information elsewhere. These chapters focus on the beliefs and behaviors, attitudes and interactions that form the fabric of life in our classrooms and in our schools. Learning can happen in isolation; teaching happens between people. Effective teaching calls for "people skills," and the best teachers practice those skills every day.

The format of this book is straightforward. An introductory chapter provides context on the importance of learning from the most effective teachers. A concluding chapter asks us to center on our own core beliefs. And in between are fourteen chapters—one dedicated to each of the fourteen things that great teachers do differently. Each of us can do everything described in this book—everything the best teachers do.

1

Why Look at Great?

We often hear that we can learn from anyone. From effective people, we learn what to do; from ineffective people, we learn what *not* to do. Although this advice contains a grain of truth, think about it: How much can we really learn from our ineffective colleagues about being an effective teacher or leader? We already know plenty about what *not* to do. Good teachers already know not to use sarcasm, not to yell at kids, not to argue with teens in front of their friends. We don't need to visit an ineffective teacher's classroom to learn this. But we can always reap good ideas from successful educators.

Look at it another way: If teaching were a true/false test, we could raise our scores by looking over the shoulder of an unsuccessful colleague and choosing the opposite answer to each question. However, working with students is never as simple as yes or no, bad or good, true or false. Teaching is more like an open-ended essay exam. It won't help much to copy from the least prepared test taker; we already know that doodling in the margins or writing "Vicky-4-Ever" won't earn points. On the other hand, although we might not agree with everything in the best essay, we could still learn from it. At the very least, we would probably see some new ideas that we could build on. As educators, we face a myriad of choices; eliminating the inappropriate options doesn't move us forward.

Here's one more example: Imagine that you have decided to build a rocket and fly to the moon. Now imagine that you have two choices about learning how to do this: You can go to NASA, or you can come by my house on a Sunday afternoon. Well, if you choose the second option, even the most diligent observation is unlikely to advance your lunar mission. Take all the notes you want: Leaning back in the recliner doesn't inspire engine design; none of the buttons on the TV remote leads to liftoff; lemonade in the shade is not rocket fuel. (Does any of this come as a surprise?)

On the other hand, if you decide to visit NASA, how will that help? You might observe that the rockets they build are bigger than your garage. Their budget looks enormous; they have more engineers. Nevertheless, you can probably learn a good deal about the processes and technology that go into a successful launch.

These examples are simplistic, but the lesson is clear. Educators who want to promote good teaching find value in examining what effective teachers do that other teachers do not.

Studying Effective Teachers

I have had the good fortune to conduct or participate in five different studies examining effective educators and schools (Whitaker 1993, Whitaker 1997, Fiore 1999, Turner 2002, Roeschlein 2002). In each study, researchers visited two different groups of schools: schools with outstanding principals and schools with less-than-stellar leaders. Although these studies yielded many insights, their greatest contribution was to focus on the question, "What do the most effective principals do that is *different*?" Without visiting less effective sites, we may not have been able to determine the variables that distinguished the effective principals.

For example, if four outstanding principals hang the same banner in the cafeteria—"All students can learn!"—I might conclude that one key to effective leadership is an inspiring banner in the lunchroom. However, if two of the less effective leaders display the same banner, I would reconsider my conclusion. The banner alone does not guarantee success. Of course, this doesn't mean that no principal should hang a banner, or that each principal must mimic every behavior of the very effective ones. But the practices of great principals *do not get in the way of* their success—and others can learn from them. A valuable component of this work was the discovery that in every setting, teachers also exhibited a wide variety of skills. In our informal observations and interviews, we began to identify differences between the more effective and the less effective teachers. Of course, we found some behaviors that showed up in most classrooms. For example, almost every teacher—from the best to the worst—takes attendance. But as we sifted through our observations, we began to compile traits of the best teachers—the variables that set them apart from their less successful peers.

One challenge in any profession is the ability to self-reflect—accurately. Those who know how they are coming across to others, how their behavior is received, work more effectively. We all struggle to achieve this self-awareness—all too often, we fall short. In the studies of principals described earlier, practically all the principals thought they were doing a good job—but only some of them were right.

In my experience, many ineffective teachers also think they are doing a good job. But like most principals, most teachers are doing the best they can—and most of the teachers I encounter are willing, even eager, to learn a better way.

I recently participated in a forum that brought together a wide variety of educators to consider the future of the teaching profession. One of the questions was, "What skills will educators need if they are to be effective in the 21st Century?" I was amazed at the responses. The long list of esoteric (and seemingly unattainable) proficiencies included a computer coordinator's understanding of technology, a lawyer's grasp of special education mandates, the wisdom to lift every student to mastery of impossibly high and ever-changing state and national standards, and the best communication skills in the school. Whew! I had knots in my stomach just listening. No wonder teachers feel so much stress.

Then I realized that we were taking the wrong approach. What we really need—*all* we really need—is for all teachers to be like the best teachers. The best teachers probably do not have a barrister's background, nor can they assemble a Pentium 4 computer out of an old soda can. But they do their jobs, and they do them well—day after day, year after year, decade after decade. They adapt to change without losing sight of what really matters. Think of it this way: If *every* teacher in a school were like the best teachers, would that be a great school? Of course it would. And if all schools had educators like the best teachers, the students who walk through their doors each day would face the 21st Century with confidence.

Many researchers—among them recently, Walsh (2001), Goldhaber and Brewer (1999), Kaplan and Owings (2002), Ferguson and Ladd (1996), Thomas (2002), Hess (2001), and Ehrenberg and Brewer (1994)—have studied effective teachers. Some have found that better teachers have more subject area expertise; others correlate effectiveness with an advanced degree; still others indicate that higher scores on teachers' tests relate to classroom success. Few of us would disagree with these findings on principle.

Yet most of us know intuitively that there is more to effective teaching than these factors. We all know effective teachers with advanced degrees and others who excel without them. High scores may be related to success, but they do not directly predict it. Knowing your subject is definitely important—and yet, what of the teachers who know their subject inside out, but fail to know their students?

This book is not about *what we know*. Many teachers know what works best. This book is about *who we are;* more directly, it is about *what we do*. Nothing in the following chapters is complicated. We all do some of these things some of the time; many of us, even most of the time. The very best teachers do these things all the time. Everything described in this book is simple—but it's not always easy.

I knew a teacher who taught fifth grade for 38 years. She was absolutely phenomenal—the teacher you wish your own children, grandchildren, nieces, and nephews could have. Her spark and energy never gave out. One day I asked her how she managed to stay inspired. She replied, "This is my 38th year teaching fifth grade, but for these students, it's the first time around."

That teacher brought her skills—especially her people skills—to bear on new experiences every day, and her students reaped the rewards. Whether we teach fifth grade or first, whether we have seventeen weeks of experience or seventeen years, we can learn from her.

2

It's People,
Not Programs

Outstanding educators know that if a school has great teachers, it is a great school. Without great teachers, the school lacks the keystone of greatness. More importantly, all their audiences take the same view. If my third-grade daughter has a great teacher, I think highly of her school. Otherwise, I see her school as less than stellar—no matter how many awards she wins, no matter how many students earn top test scores, no matter how many plaques adorn the main office. Students share this perspective; if a high-school sophomore has four great teachers each day (out of four!), then believe me, that sophomore will think the school is great. As the quality of teachers drops, so does a student's opinion of the school. All the way from kindergarten through college, the quality of the teachers determines our perceptions of the quality of the school.

It's People, Not Programs

School improvement is actually a very simple concept. However, like many simple concepts, it is not easy to accomplish. There are really two ways to improve a school significantly:

- Get better teachers.
- Improve the teachers in the school.

We can spend a great deal of time and energy looking for programs that will solve our problems. Too often, these programs do not bring the improvement or growth we seek. Instead, we must focus on what really matters. It is never about programs; it is always about people. This does not mean that no program can encourage or support improvement of people within our school; however, no program inherently leads to that improvement. Believe me, if there were such a program, it would already be in place in our schools.

Each of us can think of many innovations that were touted as *the* answer in education. Too often, we expect them to solve all our woes. When they do not, we see them as the problem. However, we must keep in mind that *programs are never the solution, and they are never the problem.* Back to basics, whole language, direct instruction, assertive discipline, open classrooms, the Baldridge model, state standards, mission statements, goal setting, site-based management: There is nothing inherently right or wrong with any of these ideas. We may have a fondness for one that has met with success, or deep-seated resentment because another has been forced down people's throats. If we take a closer look at some examples, however, we might see what effective teachers never forget. It is people, not programs, that determine the quality of a school.

How Open Classrooms Got Started

Some of you may know the true history of the open classroom movement. I do not claim any expertise about this topic—but, for what it's worth, I'll share my vision of how the concept took off.

The scene is an elementary school in Anywhere, USA. At the faculty meeting just before the start of school, the principal announces that he has good news and bad news. The good news is, enrollment is higher than anticipated. The bad news is, he needs a teacher to volunteer to teach in the old auxiliary gymnasium. Awkward silence; every teacher avoids eye contact with the principal. Finally, someone raises her hand to volunteer—and not surprisingly, it's Mrs. Smith, the school's best teacher.

Some teachers in her shoes, might block off a classroom-sized rectangle and keep the students inside it. But this dynamic teacher uses every inch of space, even creating homey nooks and crannies. Then (as often happens in rapidly growing schools), within weeks the principal makes another announcement: He needs to move another class into the gym.

After a little hemming and hawing, guess who raises her hand? The second best teacher in the school, Mrs. Jones. Together, these outstanding teachers create a phenomenal environment in that old musty gym—so much excitement, energy, and engagement in learning that it gives you goose bumps just to walk in.

Later that year, visitors to Anywhere Elementary School walk around to all the classrooms. Where do they see the best teaching and learning? That's right! In the old auxiliary gym. They conclude that open classrooms are the secret to good teaching—and the rest is history.

Ironically, the cycle has come around; now everyone looks askance at open classrooms. Granted, some teachers, especially those who lack solid classroom management skills, may struggle in this environment. What's more, the noise they and their students generate may keep anyone else from sharing space with them effectively. And yet for some of the most dynamic and creative teachers, the open classroom may easily be the *best* teaching environment.

What really energized the Anywhere Elementary School gym was the presence of excellent teachers, not the absence of walls dividing their classrooms. As educators, we must understand that programs are not solutions. We must adopt changes only if they make us better. Here is another all-too-common example involving a classroom management approach.

Assertive Discipline—the Problem or the Solution?

All of us are probably familiar with some version of assertive discipline. Typically, if a student misbehaves the teacher writes the student's name on the board. If the same student misbehaves again, the teacher puts a checkmark by the name. For each instance of inappropriate behavior, the teacher adds another checkmark. Specific, predetermined consequences apply for various numbers of checkmarks.

Some people swear by this approach; others swear at it. I have worked with many schools and districts that require assertive discipline and many that officially oppose it. I believe that these schools and districts, in viewing assertive discipline as either a solution or a problem, have lost sight of the critical factor: the teacher.

Mrs. Hamilton was the best teacher I ever worked with. I had the good fortune to spend seven years in the same school with her as an assistant principal and then principal. During that time, I made at least two hundred informal visits to her classroom. In a casual conversation just before I moved out of state to take another position, Mrs. Hamilton mentioned that she was thinking of not using assertive discipline in her class the next year. I was stunned; *I had never known* that she used assertive discipline. Why did I not know? Well, I rarely saw anyone's name on the board, and I never noticed a student's name with a checkmark beside it. Her classroom management skills were as polished as her teaching.

Mrs. Hamilton did not see assertive discipline as a necessary classroom management approach. However, if I had decided that assertive discipline was wrong and banned it in our school, would that have helped her as a teacher? If assertive discipline gave her confidence, then the students and our school were better for it.

Now, you may be thinking that assertive discipline seems to be the best approach. Of course, if this were true, every teacher would use it and thrive in their classrooms. Well, I'd like you to meet Mr. Lewis, a teacher from my first year as a principal.

In the second week of school, I decided to make the rounds of my teachers' classrooms. At twenty-six—younger than every teacher in the school—I was a little hesitant to visit classes, but I knew that this was the best way to help improve instruction. So, I walked in to Mr. Lewis's third period English class. I quickly realized that he was quite familiar with assertive discipline. On the board were the names of about a dozen students. The last one was Ricky—written in letters a foot high, with at least five checkmarks, each one larger than the one before. The last checkmark was three feet tall from point to tip. At the board, hunched over like a leprechaun, Mr. Lewis was aggressively gesturing toward the student, "Come on! You want another one!"

Clearly, assertive discipline was not working here. I might have tried to find a "better" technique, but this would merely have placed a new, equally ineffective bandage over the same gaping wound. Assertive discipline was not the problem; Mr. Lewis was the problem. On the other hand, while assertive discipline was not a problem in Mrs. Hamilton's classroom, neither was it the solution. Mrs. Hamilton was the solution.

It's Not What You Do, It's How You Do It

All teachers are aware that the students in their schools have individual needs. Educators need to be equally aware that faculty members also vary in their individual abilities and approaches. Whether the arena is classroom management or instructional techniques, effective educators focus on the people, not on the programs. They see programs as solutions only when the programs bring out the best in their teachers.

Take, for example, the whole language–phonics debate. When we took basal readers away from every teacher, we took away the support that some teachers needed just to survive in the classroom. However, by requiring all teachers to center on phonetics, we may have lost some of the best instruction that others had to offer.

Another recent example is the debate over praise and rewards for students. Like many issues, its merits cannot be decided by discussion alone. Otherwise, by now we would know whether praising or rewarding students actually motivates them to do better. Some of our best teachers praise and/or reward their students; so do some of our least effective teachers. What matters is not whether they do it, but how appropriately and effectively they do it.

The Poor Lecturer's Classroom

How many of us have ever been in a poor lecturer's classroom? Probably almost every one of us, at one time or another. When I say, "poor lecturer's classroom," which of these three words captures the problem? (I'll give you a hint—it isn't "classroom.") Most people respond, "lecturer"—but that's not right either. An effective lecturer can hold a class spellbound, delivering important information in a way that makes sense, laying the groundwork for active learning. The word that captures the problem here is "poor."

If you peeked into that classroom, you might think, "Can't the teacher see that the students are bored stiff?" Well, if her students have looked that way for 23 years, why should she catch on now? Or if his classroom is quiet for the first time all day, why should he stir things up?

But banning lectures from our classrooms won't improve our schools. The person, not the practice, needs to change. And, as we mentioned in Chapter 1, the first step may be the hardest: The teacher must recognize the need to improve.

3

The Power
of Expectations

Every teacher has a classroom to manage. One may guide a class of five girls studying advanced Latin around a well-lit seminar table; another may teach sixteen biology students in a laboratory with sparse or obsolete equipment; a third may greet twenty bouncy kindergartners every morning. I'm convinced that these three teachers—and indeed, all teachers—do the best they can when it comes to classroom management. After all, a teacher's classroom management sets the stage for student learning. We all want our students to behave well in class; if we could do anything to improve student behavior, surely we would.

How do the best teachers approach classroom management? What do they do differently? Here's the answer in a nutshell: Great teachers focus on expectations. Other teachers focus on rules. The least effective teachers focus on the consequences of breaking the rules.

Expectations

Great teachers are very clear about their approach to student behavior. They establish clear expectations at the start of the year and follow them consistently as the year progresses. For example, a teacher might have three guidelines:

Be respectful.		Respect yourself.
Be prepared.	or	Respect others.
Be on time.		Respect your school.

The teacher may have predetermined and stated consequences for misbehavior, but these are clearly secondary to
the *expectations*. The key is to set expectations and then establish relationships so that students want to meet these expectations. Great teachers don't focus on "What am I going to do if
students misbehave?" They expect good behavior—and generally that's what they get.

Rules

"School" and "rule" just seem to go together—and not
only because they rhyme. Rules establish a necessary framework for the everyday life of schools. Which of us would want
to teach in a school without rules? And yet rules have their
drawbacks. For one thing, rules in schools often focus on undesirable behaviors—with predictable results.

Stop the Thumping!

Visiting a middle school a few years ago, I was sitting in
the back of a very effective teacher's classroom. The class was
quietly focused on important projects. Suddenly, a whole-
school announcement came over the loudspeaker. Interrupt-
ing every class in the building, the principal issued the following proclamation:

> "Students in this school must immediately stop
> thumping! There have been too many students in
> the school thumping other students. Thumping is
> when you pull back your middle finger with your
> thumb and then release it so that it strikes another
> person sharply in the chest. We will have no more
> thumping in this school. Anyone caught thumping
> should be sent to the office."

Well, as I looked around the room, not one student was
still focused on the project. Instead, 29 students were practicing some form of "thumping" on themselves or on a partner.
In fact, I soon realized that I too was sitting there thumping
myself, just to see what it felt like.

Our most challenging students tend to be contrary by nature; as a matter of fact, there's a streak of the contrary in each of us. "I do not want to hear a single peep!" Who among us, hearing that, isn't tempted to peep? Or waiting, even hoping, for someone else to peep? And yet, until we heard that command, we might not have been thinking of peeping at all.

Consequences

By their very nature, rules outline the boundary between the acceptable and the unacceptable—and they attach consequences to misbehavior. We're all familiar with this from the world of competitive sports. Referees don't just point out rule violations; they assign penalties. Those who break the rules must pay the price.

The purpose of this system, of course, is to encourage players to observe the rules. Likewise, one purpose of the consequences attached to misbehavior in schools is to encourage other students to follow the school rules.

On the other hand, there are disadvantages to spelling out cut-and-dried consequences. Students are experts at cost-benefit analysis: If I skip one hour of class, I'll have to go to two hours of detention. Is it worth it? (How many of my buddies will be in detention?)

During my years as a principal, I observed that 90 percent of the students in a school have never been sent to the office. I'm willing to bet they don't have any idea what happens at the office, don't know what their parents would do if they were sent there—and would just as soon not find out. This fear of the unknown can sometimes be a more powerful deterrent than a list of predetermined consequences.

Set Expectations at the Start of the Year

A school year is a journey that takes many different turns. One of the most exciting and challenging aspects of being a teacher is that each day is so different. I love the cycle of the school year, beginning with the anticipation, excitement, and energy of the first day. Standardized testing, preholiday events, the time before and after seasonal vacations, the dark days of winter, the first days of spring—each part has its own feel, its own dynamic ebb and flow, its own highlights and challenges. A school year has a personality all its own. There is a start, a middle, and an end. Few occupations are so cyclical.

The excitement of starting a new school year provides opportunities to reestablish expectations and introduce changes. We're all on our best behavior, full of positive energy about the coming year. For effective teachers, the start of the year is a chance to set the tone for the school year and, more importantly, for the students. Even if we have been teaching the same grade or subject for several years, the opening of school is a new opportunity to move our teaching forward.

We Are Still Undefeated

Every school should have its Back-to-School Night before the year starts, or at the latest, on the evening of the first or second day of school. The reason is very simple—we are still undefeated. Students have not been "in trouble" (whatever that means). None of us are behind in our work. Nobody has any grades in the grade book. We have the chance to build new relationships. Like every major league baseball team in spring training, we can dream of making it to the World Series.

Can you see why it's so essential for teachers to establish expectations at the very beginning of the year? If we wait until the second week of school, it's much more likely that we'll be setting rules—No Thumping!—and handing out penalties for past misbehavior. If we make it clear ahead of time that we expect students to be prepared, responsible, and on time, then we can start out on the right foot and keep moving forward.

What is the variable? Not the specifics of the expectations, but that they are clearly established, focus on the future, and are consistently reinforced. All teachers can do this. The great ones do. They establish expectations for their students—and for themselves.

4

Prevention Versus Revenge

Even in the best classrooms in the best schools, with the best teachers and the best students, now and then things go wrong. In the last chapter, we looked at the power of expectations. Now we turn our attention to what one assistant principal jokingly refers to as "the dark side of the force." What do the great teachers do when a student misbehaves? What principles guide their behavior in difficult situations? How do they respond when things go wrong?

When a Student Misbehaves

When a student misbehaves, the great teacher has one goal: to keep that behavior from happening again. The least effective teacher often has a different goal: revenge. Effective teachers are motivated to prevent misbehavior; ineffective teachers are motivated *after* a student misbehaves, to punish the student. If a child does not bring a pencil to class, they want that child to feel badly about it and choose to behave better as a result. They focus on the penalty, the punishment—the past.

Think about the parents we work with. Some parents consistently look to the future. They wonder what we can do differently so that their child will be more successful. Other parents consistently focus on the past. They talk about last year's teacher, or an experience the child's older sibling went through in another setting. Some parents even harp on what happened when they themselves were in school! Which parents would *you* rather work with?

As educators, we must focus on what we have the ability to influence. We all know we can't change what has already happened; what's the point of directing our energy there?

Let's work instead to prevent the misbehavior from happening again.

Sending Students to the Office

Let's consider how teachers might want a student to behave after a disciplinary conference with the principal. Ineffective teachers want students to be upset when they leave the office. Effective teachers want students to be better when they leave. As a principal, I worked hard to help my teachers understand that we do not want students angry when they leave. Heck, they were angry when they got there. As a matter of fact, that may be why they were referred to the office in the first place. Angry students are a problem, not a solution.

Of course, teachers are entitled to support from the principal in discipline matters. But effective teachers have a clear understanding of what this support entails. I'd like to share a story that illustrates this from the principal's point of view.

"Nuthin' Happened"

One of my guidelines as a principal was that if a student cursed at a teacher, the consequence was a ten-day out-of-school suspension. One week into the new school year, one of the toughest eighth graders in the school crossed the line—and landed in my office.

When I found out what he had done, I told him he was suspended for ten days. To my surprise, he burst into tears. He was genuinely upset. Then when I called his parents, they were really ticked off—at him. "Cussing at teachers... I don't know where he gets that #@~& from!" ("Me either," I thought. "Must be cable television.")

His parents lived far from town; he would have to ride the bus home. Until then, he sat in my office and sobbed. Finally, with the last bell of the day about to ring, I offered him a box of tissues and helped him settle down. Then I escorted him to his bus.

As it happened, several of his classmates—and the teacher who had sent him to me—were standing there. I heard one of his buddies ask, "What happened when you got sent to the office?" The culprit replied, "Nuthin'," and hopped on the bus.

That won me a glare from the teacher—but as we talked about it later, it also gave us both an important insight. Of course he said, "Nuthin' happened." What was he supposed to say? "They broke me like a horse. I've been bawling like a baby for an hour! I'll never do anything wrong again!"

Effective teachers understand that what matters is not whether a student leaves the office mad, and not what the student reports to his peers, but how the student behaves in the future. Effective teachers don't need the principal to wield the sword of revenge on their behalf. They *do* need the principal to reinforce their expectations for student behavior and to support their responses to misbehavior. In fact, they welcome all the help they can get!

A Teacher's Bag of Tricks

While the support of the administrator is always helpful, here are some questions that the excellent educator asks himself/herself.

- ◆ "What can teachers do when a student misbehaves?"

  List all the options—not just what you would do, but what any teacher, good or bad, rookie or veteran, might do.

I've done this with many groups, and the lists look remarkably similar: eye contact, proximity, redirect the student, send them to the office, put them in timeout, argue with the student, send them to sit in the hall, yell, ignore, praise another student for positive behavior, embarrass them, and so on.

(Now, most of you probably flinch at some of these behaviors and nod in agreement with others. However, the point here is quantity. After we generate a list, we can shift to quality.)

Now answer this question:

- ◆ "Which of these approaches *always* work?"

The answer is clear: "None of them." Of course there is no one approach that always works. If there were, we would use it every time.

These options are a teacher's bag of tricks. Ask yourself this:

♦ "Does every teacher have the same options?"

The answer is yes. Every teacher has the same tools in their bag of tricks. Every teacher can use eye contact or proximity, send a student to the office, praise, argue, or yell. Not every teacher does, but any teacher *could* do everything on your list and any other lists teachers can generate.

What, then, is the difference between good classroom managers and poor classroom managers? It's not what is in our bag of tricks; they are all the same. What are the variables?

One variable, of course, is how often the teachers reach into their bag of tricks. A great teacher reaches in once or twice a day. A poor teacher grabs away several times an hour, and if we reach into our bag of tricks often enough, we're going to pull out some ugly ones.

This brings us to another, more important variable—the question of *quality*. Some options that often appear on the list—yelling, arguing, and humiliating (sarcasm)—deserve special attention. Ask yourself the following questions:

♦ "When is sarcasm appropriate in the classroom?"

You know the answer: *Never.* Then let's never use it in our classrooms.

♦ "Who decides how many arguments you get into in a week?"

The answer, of course, is that *we do*. We never win an argument with a student. As soon as it starts, we have lost. If their peers are watching, they cannot afford to give in. We would *like* to win the argument, but they *have* to win the argument. (Plus, I have always felt that in all student–teacher interactions, there needs to be at least one adult—and I would prefer that it be the teacher.)

♦ "Outside of a true emergency—*Watch out for the acid!*—when is an appropriate time and place for yelling?"

Again, we know the answer is *never*. The students we are most tempted to yell at have been yelled at so much, why on earth would we think this would be effective with them? Therefore, we do not yell at students.

Effective teachers choose wisely from their bag of tricks.

Respect Your Students, Their Parents—and Yourself

As educators, we know how important it is to treat students with respect, no matter how they behave. We do this for our students' sake; otherwise, they won't thrive in our classrooms. We also understand that we should extend the same respect to their parents—again, no matter how they behave; otherwise, we won't be able to work productively with them to help their child. However, there's another reason we should treat students and their parents with respect: We do it for our own sake. Think of how you feel when you know you have treated a student or parent inappropriately. Knowing that you have made them feel badly, you feel worse!

During a recent workshop on dealing with difficult parents, one teacher described a typical problem—a teacher who telephones a parent to discuss a child's misbehavior is blasted with a barrage of rudeness—and offered a simple solution: Just hang up the phone. The rest of the group sympathized with the situation; such harangues are enough to tax anyone's patience. But what happens if we choose a response like hanging up on a parent? The issue shifts from the child's behavior to our behavior. We have actually given that parent the upper hand. Especially during times of stress, it's essential to remain professional.

Twenty-Four Students
on the Side of the Teacher

It is the first day of school, and we are invisible observers in Mr. Johnson's first period social studies class. Of the twenty-five students in the room, twenty-four seem to be on their best first-day-of-school behavior. But one—we'll call him #25—is not settling in quite as well. As a matter of fact, he is downright uncooperative and rude.

At this point, assuming no other dynamics are yet established, the other twenty-four students are on Mr. Johnson's side. They want him to take steps so #25 will stop misbehaving. However, since #25 is one of them, they have special expectations. They do want #25 to stop misbehaving, but they want Mr. Johnson to deal with him in a professional and respectful way. As long as he does, they will stay on his side.

However, the first time he treats #25 in a less than professional manner—regardless of #25's behavior—the other students will side with #25. Maybe not all of them will shift their allegiance right away, but some will, and now Mr. Johnson has several #25s on his hands. If this happens often, eventually the class will consist of twenty-five #25s—and not one student on Mr. Johnson's side.

In general, students know the difference between right and wrong, and they want their teachers to deal with irresponsible peers. If you *always* respond appropriately and professionally, everyone else will be on your team. But the first time you do not, you may lose some of your supportive students—and you may never get them back. This makes maintaining a high level of dignity, especially under pressure, a critical skill. Effective teachers have this skill; others do not.

Restoring Trust

Conflict between a teacher and a student, or between a teacher and a parent—especially if it is not resolved—often leads to a loss of trust. The student or parent loses trust in the teacher; perhaps the teacher loses trust as well.

In Chapter 6, we'll look at how the best teachers take responsibility for changing situations and behaviors that have led to problems. In Chapter 9, we'll address the importance of repairing relationships that have been damaged by past missteps. Great teachers understand that any loss of trust is difficult to remedy. Even more crucially, they know that unless they work to prevent a repetition of the conflict, the fragile trust might never be restored. Our efforts to rebuild that trust are often more productive if we focus on the future more than on the past.

5

High Expectations— for Whom?

Recently I was addressing a large group of teachers. Just as I was building up to my main point, a teacher in the audience raised her hand. Although this is unusual, especially with large groups in this format, I paused and called on her. She asked, "Do you mind if we grade papers or read the newspaper while you are speaking?"

The question caught me off guard, and I reacted honestly. "I don't mind if you grade papers or read the newspaper during my presentation," I said. "I don't mind at all—as long as you are comfortable with students doing whatever they want to do in your class while you are teaching."

A ripple of laughter spread through the room, and I paused for a long moment. Then I asked the audience, "How many of you have heard that great teachers have high expectations for students?" Of course, almost everyone raised a hand.

Setting aside the thread of my presentation for a moment, I invited them to consider this statement more closely—and I invite you now to do the same.

Are High Expectations Important?

Many people believe, and I agree, that great teachers have high expectations for students. However, let's focus on the question, *what is the variable?* True, the best teachers have high expectations for students. But is this a *difference* that separates great teachers from the rest?

Even the *worst* teachers have high expectations for students. They expect students to be engaged no matter how irrelevant the material is. They expect students to pay attention no matter how boring and repetitious their classes are. They expect students to be well behaved no matter how the teacher treats them. Now, *those* are high expectations.

The variable is not what teachers expect of students; many teachers of all skill levels have high expectations for students. The variable—and what really matters—is *what teachers expect of themselves*. Great teachers have high expectations for students but even higher expectations for themselves. Poor teachers have high expectations for students but much lower expectations for themselves. Not only that, they have unrealistically high expectations for everyone else as well. They expect the principal to be perfect, every parent to be flawless, and every one of their peers to hold them in incredibly high regard.

I turned back to the teacher whose question had sparked this discussion. As a presenter, I said, I feel a responsibility to engage the audience. I believe that what I am saying is important, and of course I want my audience to give me their full attention—but it's my job to gain, and to keep, their attention. If I'm not doing that, I need to change my approach.

Just like in the classroom, we must always work to engage the students. If the students are not focused, great teachers ask what they themselves can do differently.

Before I returned to my presentation, I posed a challenge to the teachers in the room. It's easy to have high expectations for the students in your classrooms, I said. The challenge is to focus on your own performance. Strive to be a great teacher; set even higher expectations for yourself.

6

Who Is the Variable?

What really makes the difference between two schools? What matters most in the classroom? Effective educators understand the answer to these questions; indeed, they know that the real issue is not *what* is the variable, but *who*. Great teachers know who is the variable in the classroom: They are.

Who Is the Variable in the Classroom?

How many of you could predict which teacher in your school will send the most students to the office next year? How about the year after that? When I ask a roomful of principals this question, pretty much every hand goes up. I then ask, "How can you possibly know this? Do you already have the student rosters made up?" The answer is very simple: They know because the main variable in a classroom is *not* the students. The main variable is the teacher.

Interestingly, when I ask any group of teachers this question, they have the same response. (Generally the only teachers who don't raise their hands are the two or three who send the most students to the office.) Now, if we all know this, we ought to be able to talk about it. I have always believed that if there is an elephant in the room, it's important to acknowledge its presence—not just tiptoe around it, pretending it isn't there. Understand, that does not mean we attack the portly pachyderm, or make fun of it—just that we recognize it and take steps to deal with it.

What If the Students Do Poorly?

Ask yourself these questions:

- ◆ If the best teacher in a school gives a quiz, test, or homework assignment and the students do poorly on it (and, as we are all aware, this can happen to the best of us), whom does she blame?

  The predictable answer: *Herself.*

- ◆ Now, if the worst teacher in a school gives a quiz, test, or homework assignment and the kids do poorly on it (and, as we just acknowledged, this can happen to the best of us), whom does he blame?

- ◆ Predictable answers: *The kids, or the parents, or the administration ("If we had some discipline around here maybe we could teach these kids something"), or last year's teachers, or drugs, or MTV, or...*

- ◆ Whose behavior can a teacher actually control in his classroom?

  The only possible answer: *His own.*

The answers speak for themselves.

What is the variable here? Not the students doing poorly on the assignment; that happens in both groups. The variable is *how the teachers respond.* Good teachers consistently strive to improve, and they focus on something they can control—their own performance. Other teachers wait for something else to change. Great teachers look to themselves for answers; poor teachers look elsewhere. As we know, they can wait a very long time for anything else to make a difference.

Clearly, the best teachers accept responsibility for their classrooms and the worst teachers do not. I do a great deal of work in classroom management. When I talk to teachers about behavior issues, whose behavior do you think I talk about? The teacher's, of course. Otherwise, it's all too easy to feel overwhelmed and defeated. When we center on our own behavior, we feel empowered to make a difference.

At all levels of our school systems, the effective educators take responsibility. Some superintendents blame the school board for their woes; others work to educate its members. Some teachers lament, "This is the worst group of students I've ever had!" Others rise to the challenge of making every class their best. Most educators have had the feeling, at one time or another, that they are at the bull's-eye of a community's concerns. The great teachers place themselves in the bull's-eye.

How Do We Deal With the Demands of Others?

This concept of accepting responsibility is not limited to education, although at times it may seem so. We constantly hear or read criticisms of schools and teachers. To survive, we must put these in context. Others, including our critics, focus on their own situations and needs. By the same token, everyone's effectiveness depends at least in part on what they expect of themselves, not of others.

A few years ago, the chamber of commerce in my community held a meeting whose purpose was billed as "enhancing dialogue and communication between businesses and education." The superintendent asked me, as a principal, and two teachers in my school to represent the school district. I was flattered—until we walked into the room. Around a large circular table sat approximately 15 business "leaders." The three of us were the only representatives from the education community.

To start the conversation, the business leaders shared their perceptions of "the problem with education nowadays." One by one, they vented their frustrations. "We hire these people and they can't add or subtract," whined the first one. His buddy chimed in, "We hire these people and they can't read or write." The litany went on and on: "We hire these people and their attendance is terrible," "We hire these people and they can't get along with authority." What a treat for my teachers and me!

After about 25 minutes, it finally got to me. I spoke from the heart.

"Your concerns seem to be following a pattern. We hire these people and they can't add or subtract, read or write, show up on time, follow instructions…"

The business leaders nodded aggressively.

I looked at them and asked, "Who hires these people?"

I went on: "I used to be a high school counselor, and I never received one call from a potential employer requesting a reference for a student. If you need a way to determine whether an applicant can add and subtract, we can provide old-fashioned worksheets to do that in fifteen minutes. But that's not my biggest issue. What is the variable here?"

I was on a roll. They had touched a core belief of mine—accepting responsibility—and I wasn't about to let them get away with holding others to a higher standard than they applied to themselves.

"How come, with four McDonalds in town, two have great service and two have very rude employees? Ask for help in one of the grocery stores—on the east side of town, you'll get a friendly smile, and on the west side you'd think you were offering someone a root canal. What makes the difference? All six of these stores hire from the same pool of candidates. All of them pay the same wages. *What is the variable?*"

"We all know the answer: It's the effectiveness of those who are managing the businesses. And, amazingly, those effective managers assume *it is up to them* to hire and train quality employees—just as the effective teachers assume they are responsible for the students in their classes, even though they have no voice in selecting them."

"Now, instead of blaming, let's see how we can work together so that all of us can be more productive and effective in what we do."

Whew! I needed to say that—and to their credit, they listened.

Accepting responsibility is an essential difference between more effective and less effective employers, teachers, principals—even parents. (Which parents take responsibility for setting expectations about their children's behavior? Which are quickest to blame others?) As teachers, we must examine our own acceptance of responsibility. More than that: We must help all teachers take responsibility for their performance in the classroom. If everyone looks in the mirror when they ask, "Who is the variable?" we will have made tremendous strides toward school improvement. This empowering approach raises the level of teacher efficacy and will eventually be passed on to students. Success in any profession starts with a focus on self. After all, we are the one variable that we can most easily and most productively influence.

7

Ten Days out of Ten

One of the hallmarks of effective teachers is that they create a positive atmosphere in their classrooms and schools. So many things can bring teachers down: an upset parent, a troubled student, limited resources. These are facts of the job (and of life). As educators, our role is to take a positive approach—ten days out of ten.

Effective teachers treat everyone with respect, every day. Even the best teachers may not like all their students—but they act as if they do. And great teachers understand the power of praise.

We Never Forget That One Time

It's not difficult to treat *some* people with respect, or even to treat *most* people with respect. It's even possible to treat *all* people with respect quite a bit of the time. The real challenge is to treat everyone with respect every day. Each of us can remember at least one occasion in our professional lives when someone in a leadership role treated us inappropriately. No matter how long ago it was, or how often that person treated us well, we remember. The same thing is true in our schools. If just once in a month, or even once in a year, we choose to make a sarcastic comment or cutting remark to a student or colleague, we might as well have carved it in stone. They may pretend to have forgotten that moment, but they will never forget. What's more, anyone else who witnessed it will probably remember too.

You Do Not Have
to Like the Students

In my talks to educators, I often give this example from my years as a principal. Every year, it was my practice to remind my faculty: "You don't have to *like* the students; you just have to *act as if* you like them." The reason is simple; if you don't act as if you like them, then it doesn't matter how much you like them. And if you act as if you like them, then whether you like them at all becomes irrelevant.

Think of the teachers you most admire. Do they like some of their students less than others? Of course they do. But ask yourself this: How do they treat the students they like least? Well, the best teachers treat them just like all the other students. Every student might as well be their favorite student. Whether they like a student or not, they *act as if* they do.

Now think of the worst teachers you have known. Surely they had students they liked—some better than others—but from their behavior, you would think they didn't like any students very much at all! Our behaviors are much more obvious than our beliefs. We will expand on this concept a little later in the book, but it is important in the context of how we treat people every day of the year.

The Power of Praise

Effective teachers treat their students with positive regard. In particular, effective teachers understand the power of praise.

Learning how to praise may be a challenge for many of us. As teachers, we find it all too easy to spend our time looking for what is wrong, pointing out errors, and focusing on mistakes. However, an effective teacher looks for opportunities to find people doing things right and knows how to praise those people so they'll keep on doing things right.

Five Things That Help Praise Work

Ben Bissell (1992) has described five things that help praise work—elements that are important if attempts at praise are to have their most positive effect. To be effective, praise must be *authentic, specific, immediate, clean,* and *private.* Let us apply these general characteristics to the specifics of motivating and praising in our daily life.

First—*Authentic* means that we are praising people for something genuine, recognizing them for something that is true. This is an important facet because the recognition of something authentic can never grow weary. Sometimes people state that they do not praise more because they feel that it will lose its credibility or that it will become less believable if it happens too much. The way to prevent this is to make sure that it is always authentic. No one ever feels that they are praised too much for something genuine. Authentic does not mean that it is earth-shattering or that it is a magnificent accomplishment. The only requirement is that it be true. You don't need to wait until your friend loses 55 pounds before you compliment him. He won't mind hearing that he's looking good after just ten days of puffing around the track! (In fact, that may be when he most needs to hear it.) As educators, we have many opportunities to catch people doing things right. Each is an opportunity to give authentic praise.

Second—Effective praise is *specific.* The behavior we acknowledge often becomes the behavior that will be continued. If we can recognize others' positive efforts with specific appreciation, then we can help them recognize the value of these efforts as well. For example, acknowledging that a student did an effective job of asking questions during a class period can help reinforce this learning skill. Specific praise also allows you to reinforce someone in an authentic manner. If you use specific praise, you can recognize everyone in your classes—even students who are struggling. You do not have to be dishonest and say that a person is outstanding academically, or that a paper is excellent, if that's not the case. Instead, you can identify those areas that did have merit and acknowledge them through praise.

I am reminded of a student named Aaron, who was walking down the hallway one February day. I was principal at the time, and I noticed that Aaron was wearing a new sweater. (I saw Aaron in my office often enough that I pretty much knew his entire wardrobe.) As Aaron drew near I said to him, "Boy, Aaron, that is a good-looking sweater you've got on there." Aaron hadn't had much occasion to smile at me before, but he cracked a smile that morning. Not only that—he wore that sweater to school every day for the next three weeks, and made sure I noticed it! Every one of us appreciates authentic, specific praise.

Third—*Immediate praise*. This means recognizing positive efforts and contributions in a timely manner. Providing authentic and specific feedback when good things happen, or soon afterward, is an important element in making reinforcement effective. We are so fortunate in education—we have dozens of opportunities every day to give immediate feedback to those around us. If a student tries extra hard, or a class puts on a program that really sparkles, or a couple of our colleagues spend their break tidying up the faculty room, we can say right away, "Nice job!" And the more often we do this, the more praise becomes a habit.

Fourth—praise must be *clean*. This is often a very challenging expectation, especially for educators. Clean means a couple of different things.

First, praise is not clean if you are issuing it to get someone to do something in the future. In other words, it is important to compliment someone because it is authentic, not just because you are hoping that they will do something different—and unrelated—tomorrow. Take care to remind yourself of this quite regularly; otherwise, you will be tempted to discontinue praising because you feel it "did not work." For example, you might praise a student's homework assignment on Monday; on Friday, that student might blurt out yet another rude comment during class. Do not feel that these two events are linked. Oftentimes we take the inappropriate behavior of less positive students too personally. Although our goal is to get them to be more positive, we need to be aware that more often their mood has much more to do with the way they feel about themselves than it does with how they regard us.

The second aspect of clean praise is also tricky for educators: If praise and reinforcement is to be clean, it cannot include the word "but." If we are trying to compliment a student and we say, "I appreciated the work you did on your math today, but you need to finish your social studies assignment," the individual we hoped to praise will very likely only remember the part after the "but"—which was a criticism.

If we really intend to praise someone, then it is important that we separate these two comments. "I appreciated the work you did on your math today" could have been an authentic, specific, immediate, positive, and reinforcing event for that student. Such a statement helps to clarify and reinforce our expectations about how students should complete work. It also makes it much more likely that the student will consciously seek to work this way in the future. The other part of the comment, "you need to finish your social studies assignment," should be given at another time and in another way. Tying the two together reduces or even eliminates the value of the praise. ("You're looking trim these days, Joe, but I've been wondering what has happened to your hair"—which part of that sentence has lasting impact?)

Finally, effective praise is *private.* Dr. Bissell believes that the vast majority of the time, praise needs to be given in private. I agree with this and would also say that if in doubt, you are always safe to praise someone in private. Remember the old days when teachers would say, "I am giving back the tests from best to worst. Jimmy, come on up and get yours first." Often the end result of this is either that Jimmy makes sure he never gets the best grade again, or that the other students make sure to take out their frustration on Jimmy at recess.

Likewise, recognizing students publicly when they get a 3.5 grade point average may seem reinforcing, but many of these students would rather receive private recognition; it may not be "cool" to have high grades. Having a private ceremony for these "honor roll" students, or sending their parents a letter, would probably accomplish the same thing without potentially building resentment among their peers. Realistically, we often have many students in our schools who could not have achieved this lofty GPA, and no amount of watching others garner praise is likely to launch them onto the honor roll.

However you elect to reinforce the efforts of others, it is essential that you *Raise the Praise!* on a regular basis. Nobody minds hearing praise. As a matter of fact, if we praise correctly *it is impossible to praise too much.* And if you question this, just think: Have you ever been praised too much? Of course not. You may have been falsely flattered by someone you knew was not genuine, but if the praise is authentic, it's never too much.

When I work with teachers, I often remind them that how much we praise is a choice. And what's more, every time I praise someone, at least two people feel better—and one of them is *me*. Then why are educators so hesitant to praise? Here are some of the most common responses I get from principals and teachers when I ask why they do not praise more. Let's examine this thinking.

- *Reason:* If I praise people, they will stop working.

  Response: If students say how much they enjoy your class, do you slack off and show a video the next day? No, you try even harder. Which comment is more likely to keep you on a diet: "You're looking good," or "It's about time"? If a neighbor compliments you on the lawn you just mowed, do you mow it less carefully next time? Quite the opposite. Next time you might even trim! If you question whether praise works, come on over to my house and look at—my neighbor's lawn.

Authentic praise is a powerful reinforcer and motivator.

- *Reason:* If I start praising people, I might miss someone and hurt their feelings.

  Response: Is it better never to praise anyone? If we miss everyone, whose feelings do we spare? And maybe it's not *their* feelings we are worried about; perhaps *we* don't want to feel badly because we left someone out, or perhaps we are unsure of their response so we don't take a chance. People who resent praise given to others do so mainly because they don't feel valued themselves. The solution is not less praise, but a much more inclusive and generous effort to recognize others. Praise is one key to working effectively with high achievers.

♦ *Reason:* I don't have the time.

Response: After all, we barely have time to get in all the griping, whining, and complaining we need to do, now don't we? (Sorry, was that sarcasm?) Now (excluding yourself), name the three teachers in your school who praise the most. Now, name the three best teachers in your school. Is there any overlap there?

I don't know about you, but I would love to be treated the way the best teachers treat their students. Getting called *sir* or *ma'am*, always hearing *please* and *thank you*, and consistently being treated with respect and dignity sounds awfully nice to me.

The teacher who sets a positive tone can influence the interactions of everyone in the school. We must make sure we do this even when we least feel like it (and remember, praising others helps us to feel like it). Focusing on all of the positive things in our classrooms and schools—and there are many—gives us more drive and energy to get through the less positive times. If we do not set this positive tone, who will? And if we do not establish a productive focus, should we be surprised if the voices of the nay sayers set quite a different tone?

Too Much Nice

I know that everyone reading this book faces a multitude of demands—and they are growing. Special education, alternative education, drug-free education, sex education, and of course the new state standards—all affect our schools and our responsibilities. Each of these may even be essential. We could debate forever about whether we have enough of one or too much of another. But I know one thing for sure: We never have *too much nice*.

Effective educators understand that one of a teacher's most important tasks is to model appropriate behavior. With all the challenges we face in school, and sometimes at home, being nice to others may seem trivial; but if our classrooms and schools can have that as a foundation, many of the other challenges become less daunting. Teachers who consistently model their expectations for how people should be treated give their schools a valuable gift—a gift that, in time, everyone in the school can give to each other.

If everyone in a school is treated with respect and dignity you may still have nothing special. However, if everyone in a school is not treated with respect and dignity you will never have anything special. Of that, I am sure.

8

The Teacher Is the Filter

Teachers are the filters for the day-to-day reality of school. Whether we are aware of it or not, our behavior sets the tone. If students overhear us whining or complaining about something, it may be the talk of the school for days even if it was something minor. By the same token, if we always approach things in a positive manner, then this is what the students reflect. The most effective educators understand this and choose their filters carefully.

How Is Your Day Going?

As educators, we hear this question many times a day. Our response not only influences how others view us, but also affects the frame of mind of the person who asked. What's more, we have choices about how to respond.

You can smile at a fellow teacher and say, "Things are great! How about with you?" Or you can respond, "That Jimmy Wallace is getting on my nerves!"—and all of a sudden Jimmy Wallace is getting on that teacher's nerves too (whether the teacher knows him or not).

You may be thinking that you could not do this because you would never lie. Hmm: So when the second graders ask if you like the mural they drew, what do you tell them? How do you answer the question, "Honey, do these pants make me look fat?" Again, it is always up to us to determine what gets through our filters and what does not.

The Angry Parent

Here's one scenario, filtered two ways. Let's examine what happens under each. Say I'm a homeroom teacher, meeting with an irate parent behind closed doors. As so often happens, Mrs. Smith is really mad at the world; I just happen to be the one sitting there as she vents her feelings. After she leaves, I walk into the hall and a colleague says innocently, "How is your day going?" Now I have choices to make.

I can choose to filter my response: "Things are great, how about with you?" If that teacher feels good about the world, we both move on, smiling. If he has concerns, at least I have not made them worse.

Or I can respond, "Oh, I just met with that whacko parent Mrs. Smith. Man, she has some temper! I hope I never have to deal with her again. Yikes!" Now, what have I accomplished? Well, I have made that teacher terrified of Mrs. Smith. And if I tell enough people about Mrs. Smith, I might have every teacher in the school worrying about the possibility of meeting this notorious harridan. Some might be leery of working with any student whose last name is Smith, or hesitant about calling any parents (and especially the ones named Smith). I have shifted their energy away from confidently approaching their students to unproductive worrying.

One way or the other, my response affects the school. By sparing others the unnecessary bad news, I can create a much more productive environment.

When the Teacher Sneezes

When the teacher sneezes, the whole class catches a cold. This is neither good nor bad; it is just the truth. Our impact is significant; our focus becomes the student's focus. If we have great credibility and good relationships, students work to please us. If we lack credibility, students work against us. Students come to class each day wanting and expecting us to set the tone. If the tone we establish is positive and professional, they'll match that tone; if our attitude is negative and confrontational, they'll respond in kind.

We often hear the statement, "You have to earn students' respect." Yet the students are on their best behavior the first day of school. Did we earn that? Did we work with the students and their families one on one over the summer to build that bond? Of course not. On the first day of school, students hand us respect on a platter. We determine what happens to that gift. The best teachers continue to nurture and build respect all year long.

One Goal, Every Day

I really like faculty meetings; I always have. As a principal, I cherished the opportunity to spend time with an outstanding group of professionals. I tried not to waste that precious time on administrative or logistical announcements. I sought to end each meeting on a positive note, sending teachers to their next challenge with energy and enthusiasm. No matter what the purpose, content, or focus of the faculty meeting might be, I always had one fundamental goal: *I wanted the teachers to be more excited about teaching tomorrow than they were today.*

Great teachers take the same approach in their classes. No matter what the lesson plan "covers," great teachers want their students *to be more excited about learning tomorrow than they are today.*

A friend of mine once shared a story that took place in a kindergarten classroom. At the start of class, the teacher said to the students, "I think we will be inside at recess today, because it was raining on my way to work." After a pause, one of her little charges raised his hand and asked, "Where do you work?"

Each day, we decide what to bring into our classrooms. Even on the days we don't feel quite so perky, we can filter out the negative energy that makes students feel we're just there to do our job. If our attitude shows we want to be there, our students will reflect that positive energy back to us.

Where the Elite Meet?

Now and then, I ask a group of teachers, "What advice would you give a student teacher about the teachers' lounge at your school?" The most common reply is, "Stay out!" Isn't that a shame?

I don't know of a single college program that includes a class on griping in the teachers' lounge—yet some first-year teachers seem to have it down by November. Where do they pick up that habit?

Probably the best predictor of whether teachers will gripe in the teachers' lounge tomorrow is whether they heard we were griping in there today. The great teachers don't add to the litany of complaints. Instead, they filter them out.

The lounge should be a place where teachers relax, socialize, and enjoy each other's company. The faculty workroom should be a place where professionals support each other. Sure, teachers are overworked and underpaid—but do we really want to focus on those aspects of our profession during our free minutes? Teaching is a demanding job—but it's the job we've chosen, and we can choose to focus on its rewards and challenges in a positive way. The great teachers do that.

The World Outside School

It almost goes without saying that great teachers establish an effective filter between their personal lives and their classrooms. Every teacher ought to model this professional behavior. The classroom is no place to discuss marital problems, to complain about low salaries for teachers, or even to show home movies of the family pet's antics.

By the same token, the best teachers keep school issues in their place. I recently worked with a high school that was debating whether to initiate block scheduling. Teachers had strong opinions on both sides of the issue. What caught my attention, though, was the ferocity of the student involvement. In some classes, the teachers actively lobbied for or against the change. Some encouraged their students to initiate petitions, or drummed up parent attendance at school board meetings. Other teachers never brought up the issue in their classrooms; if the subject did come up, they addressed it calmly. Instead of fanning the flames of controversy, the best teachers had a quieting influence.

This Is the Worst
Group of Kids We've Ever Had

Have you ever heard this refrain? It seems that the same two or three teachers start the chant at about the same time each year. They are tired; the honeymoon with their students has long been over; they have not developed the critical positive relations in their classrooms when February and March roll around. Such complaining doesn't help to solve the problem—and indeed, in my experience such statements usually have no basis in fact.

After a recent evening of parent conferences, I heard a teacher complain, "They only care about their child!" I chuckled to myself, wondering which children she expected the parents to care about. (When you take your car to the mechanic, do you care much whether the car in the next bay gets fixed that day?) Would that teacher prefer to confer with parents who *don't* care about their child?

Whenever I hear someone complain about "this group of kids," I think again of the auto mechanic. "Sorry, sir, I wasn't able to fix your car—due to budget cuts, all the auto shops have a really high car-to-mechanic ratio this year." Would that excuse make the customer feel better? "This is the worst group of cars I've ever had!" I don't know about you, but at that point I'd start looking for another mechanic.

Perception Can Become Reality

As educators, we understand that perceptions can become reality. People who say, "This is the worst group of kids," soon start to believe it. Eventually, they start to treat them that way—and unfortunately, the students will start to behave accordingly.

Effective educators understand that one of the best ways to alter perceptions is to provide other perceptions. I'll give you an example from my first year as a principal.

I was hired in July. I had not met any of the teachers. When I started working regularly, teachers began to drop by the office. One by one, they complained about the student body: "The worst group of kids we've ever had." I was scared to death to start the school year. I remember thinking that these students must really be different than any other students in the world. I guess I was right; as I walked around the school and visited classes the first day, I realized that these students were so bad, they must have even skipped the first day!

Of course, they were there, and they were no different than the challenging students we all know. Yet I realized that the teachers' *perceptions* were an indication how they felt about the students and, ultimately, about teaching. If I could not change these perceptions, before long they would become reality. I pondered what to do.

About a month into the school year, I attended the annual state conference. One session, billed as a roundtable discussion, turned out to be a gripe session for principals, each relating their "biggest problem." I happened to sit next to the principal from a very wealthy school—we'll call it Country Club High. Well, I had always assumed that Country Club High could not possibly have problems. After all, they always had outstanding test scores, partly because of their clientele. Their sports teams were consistently winners, and their salaries were the highest in the state. Imagine my surprise when their leader described his school's biggest problem as students "pantsing" drugs—putting drugs in their underwear so that they could not be searched. That really put things in perspective for me. I resolved to share this perspective with the teachers at my school.

At the next faculty meeting I told the story. When I reported that I sat next to the principal of Country Club High, the faculty gasped as if I'd met a famous movie star. Then I told them that students at the most prestigious school in the state routinely hid drugs in their underwear. My staff was speechless. Finally, I described the biggest problem at our school: The door to Dennis Newton's locker keeps sticking. Though they chuckled at my obvious attempt to downplay our issues, the teachers realized that many of the challenges posed by "the worst group of kids we've ever had" were closer to Dennis' locker-door problem than they were to "pantsing" drugs.

We are very fortunate to work in education; sometimes we just forget how blessed we are. By consistently filtering out the negatives that don't matter and sharing a positive attitude, we can create a much more successful setting. Consciously or unconsciously, *we decide* the tone of our classrooms and of our school.

9

Don't Need to Repair—Always Do Repair

In Chapter 7, we discussed treating everyone with respect and dignity every day. This is the standard that we must all work toward, and the very best teachers come close. By the same token, most of us have worked with or for someone who was nice most of the time but would let the volcano erupt now and then. Unfortunately some of these tantrums may have resulted in personal hurts that never totally healed.

When we, as educators, lapse into such behaviors, we may never know the damage we have caused. If we become impatient and unprofessional, we are much more likely to throw darts. Though we may get over it, our targets may not. Sure, the students may still act polite toward us. After all, what choice do they have?—especially if they fear being treated like that again. However, the relationship may never be the same. Effective teachers understand this, so they aim to treat people with respect ten days out of ten. They know that a relationship, once damaged, may never be the same. That is one reason that effective educators—both principals and teachers—are so acutely sensitive to every single thing they say and do. They work to avoid actions that cause hurt feelings. The most effective among us go beyond that.

Some *Never* Need to Repair—But *Always* Do

One of the things I notice about the best teachers is that they seldom engage in the behaviors that cause harm to students. They don't make cutting remarks or issue smart retorts. They don't run students down or embarrass them in front of their peers. Quite the opposite: The best teachers consistently compliment and praise students. Yet, though the best teachers seldom need to do any emotional repairing in their class-rooms, they are continually working to repair, just in case.

Picture the most dynamic teachers in your school. They are the ones who are most likely to start off their class on a Tuesday morning by apologizing about something they did on Monday: "Class, I am sorry if I seemed a little impatient yesterday. I wasn't feeling well and I was running late. I want to let you know that I am sorry if I was a little short to any of you."

The class, of course, is sitting there with blank stares. They thought yesterday's class was great—actually, the best class they had all day. This shows not only the teacher's incredible sensitivity, but also the level of trust and credibility estab-lished with students. As we noted before, the best teachers have high expectations for others, but much higher expecta-tions for themselves. The best educators work hard to keep their relationships in good repair—to avoid personal hurt and to repair any possible damage—and others notice.

Let's contrast this approach with that of the less effective teachers and principals.

Some *Always* Need to Repair—But *Never* Do

Think about the less skilled teachers in your school. Pic-ture the ones who are most confrontational. Visualize their mannerisms, body language, and tone of voice. How do they treat the students when they are in a bad mood? Think of how they tread on students' feelings and self-worth. (Sorry to put *you* in a bad mood, but we needed to have specific individuals in mind.) Now, do they ever treat people, either students or adults, in a way that might hurt someone's feelings? Do they ever need to do some repair work? Of course. Unfortunately, you know this, and so does everyone else in their classrooms and in the school. The only ones who probably don't know this are the offenders themselves.

Intentionally or not, people like this regularly offend and insult others. Their reasons may not be as significant as their actions, especially to the person they just affronted. Yet these same individuals seldom recognize the need to repair. And more significantly, they seldom work to repair.

This has two implications. First, instead of focusing on getting them to admit they were wrong or forcing them to apologize, we really need to put our time and energies into helping build their "people skills." Otherwise, they will constantly wrestle with the issue of repair. We must center our efforts on changing their approach so that they do not need to repair.

Second, however, we want to make it easier for them to repair. What keeps them from apologizing? Usually, what stands in the way is their lack of self-confidence or—often the flip side of the same coin—their pride or ego. We may not be able to deal with these issues directly, but if we can find a way that enables them to apologize, then we can change their behaviors without necessarily altering their beliefs. Let's take a look at one method.

I Am Sorry That Happened

In the book *Dealing with Difficult Parents (And with Parents in Difficult Situations)*, I describe a tool that an educator can use to defuse aggressive parents. No matter what the details of a situation, an educator can tell the parent, "I am sorry that happened." And the amazing thing is, it's really true. Any time I deal with a belligerent parent, regardless of the issue, I truly am sorry that it happened (whatever "it" is).

I am not saying it was my fault; I am not accepting or placing blame; I am just sorry that it happened. And the more offensive the parent is, the more sorry I am it happened! To myself I am adding, "I sure am sorry it happened, otherwise I wouldn't be spending this time with you!" Of course we would never share our private thoughts with these people, and we must always maintain a professional attitude. This is also a type of filtering. Nevertheless, the simple statement "I am sorry that happened" is a powerful defusing technique.

Of course, this is not limited to parents. Any time anyone shares bad news with me, I really am sorry it happened. If a colleague's grant application is turned down, "I am so sorry that happened." If a child falls and skins her knee, "I am so sorry that happened." Again, I am not saying that I tripped her, I am just sorry it happened.

Every teacher reading this book may already know and use this approach. But the real challenge is not developing and practicing this skill ourselves, but *teaching students and other teachers* the skill. If they learn to use it regularly, they will have to do a lot less repairing in the future. In particular, if our most negative students and teachers can master this skill, what a service to them—and to us and to our school.

So, we might start by suggesting that if a parent is attacking a teacher, regardless of the circumstances that teacher should be able to say, professionally and with empathy, "I am so sorry that happened." With our most resistant colleagues, we might share a little more of our internal dialogue. If they need to add *to themselves*, "because otherwise I wouldn't be spending my time with you," that's okay. After all, they don't need to like the parent—they only need to act that way. They can even add *to themselves*, "as a matter of fact, I am a little sorry you moved into our district!" This is probably something we have all felt at times.

Of course, we must emphasize that as professionals, we can *never* be sarcastic or demeaning in our tone of voice or body language. However, on the inside we can be whatever we want. After all, what we most need these less positive teachers to do is to change their behavior. And if they change for selfish reasons, that doesn't matter. The critical issue isn't *why*, but *whether* they changed their behavior.

As a principal, I made an effort to develop and refine these skills in every staff member. But beyond that, we can reap great benefits if we teach them to our students.

The Highway Patrol

We have identified skills that we know are important to being a successful professional. As educators, we need to work to develop these abilities in our students. Some of our students have them to some degree, but many have not been exposed to them at all. For them, teachers who regularly practice the skill of repairing can serve as an important role model. But in addition to modeling the skill, we may also need to teach it.

As a principal, I had many opportunities to teach this skill. Think of all the students who are referred to the office for being uncooperative or argumentative with a teacher. Now, with all discipline matters, it is essential that we focus on prevention, not punishment. We can't do anything about the fact that the incident occurred; all we can do is try to keep it from happening again. However, we do know that each student can work to repair the current situation. This is our opportunity to help them learn how repairing relations can be to *their* advantage.

Here's a scenario:

> Johnny gets sent to my office out of Mrs. Smith's class. When he arrives, I ask him, "Johnny, what happened?" He responds that Mrs. Smith sent him to the office for arguing with her. The referral form he brought confirms his story. "Was Mrs. Smith mad?" Johnny affirms the obvious, "Yeah, she was real mad." This is my opportunity to share with Johnny the story of the highway patrol.
>
> "Johnny, I am not going to decide your consequence until I go and talk to Mrs. Smith in person." (This sound practice should be a habit in your school. It is part of making teachers *feel* supported.) "And Johnny, I won't have a chance to see her until after lunch. So, if I were in your shoes, when the bell rings at the end of this class period I would hightail it down to Mrs. Smith's classroom and I'd apologize. I would say something like," (giving Johnny the *specific* language to use) "Mrs. Smith, I am sorry that...."

Why must I give Johnny the word-for-word language? Because he may not have it himself. Telling someone to do something without teaching him how makes no sense at all. So I teach him what to say. Now, how do I actually get him to do it? Simple: I make it a benefit to *him* to do it.

I continue with the dialogue.

"And Johnny, I'm not asking you to go and apologize for my sake. And you don't even have to apologize for Mrs. Smith's sake. It's up to you—but if I were you, I would apologize for your *own* sake." "For me?" Johnny asks. "Yes, for you." This is where the highway patrol comes in.

"If I am driving down the highway and I get pulled over by a patrolman, when that patrolman is walking toward my car I have one goal. What is that goal?"

"To get out of the ticket."

"That's right. And I have two choices in my behavior: I can be nice, or I can be rude. Which is more likely to get me out of the ticket?"

"Being nice."

"And you know that my goal in being nice is selfish. It isn't to help the state revenue department. It isn't to help the highway patrolman. It is to help *me*—by making it more likely I will get out of the ticket. So if I were you, when that bell rings I'd scoot on down to Mrs. Smith's class and I would say something like..." (I give him the language again, just to ensure that he has it.)

"And you said Mrs. Smith was mad, didn't you?"

"Yep, real mad."

"Well, if you want to see her mad again, just tell her that you're apologizing because I told you to. Now you do what you want, but if I were in your shoes I'd head down to Mrs. Smith's class when that bell rings and I would apologize."

The bell rings, and guess what Johnny does? He heads down to Mrs. Smith and apologizes. When I see her after lunch, I ask what happened with Johnny. She says that he came down and apologized and everything is fine. Whose job just got easier? Mine, of course!

Now I may still need to give Johnny a consequence, because 25 other students saw his behavior. Yet he can still be reinforced by saying, "Because you apologized I am only going to…" This way I still encourage the apology. And what if Johnny doesn't go and see Mrs. Smith? I've lost nothing. It didn't work this time, but it might work in the future.

If principals and teachers take the opportunity to teach students the *behaviors* that repair a situation instead of escalating it, our jobs become easier—and their lives become better. After all, no matter what professions our students enter, they will probably need to deal with supervisors; the way they respond could determine whether they succeed in that job. (To say nothing of their encounters with the highway patrol.)

Some students already have the skill of repairing. A student who has spent the last ten minutes of chemistry class with his head on the desk might stop on his way out of class to explain that he had to work late at his after-school job. A student who has snickered during a classmate's presentation may apologize on his own. Effective teachers reinforce these behaviors; they also take advantage of teachable moments to help other students build the skill of repairing.

Furthermore, effective teachers don't wait for problems or confrontations to arise before they begin this endeavor. Educators have developed an abundance of materials designed to introduce and strengthen the skills of conflict resolution in students from pre-school to high school and beyond. When effective teachers bring these exercises to life in their classrooms, they do more than alleviate classroom discipline problems and prepare their students for success in the work environment. These great teachers help to build a more peaceful world.

10

Ability to Ignore

Great teachers have an incredible ability to ignore. This doesn't mean they are oblivious—great teachers are aware of almost everything that happens in their classrooms. Nor does it mean that they have vast reserves of patience (although that helps). Rather, it reflects their mastery of the situations that arise daily in the life of schools. They know how easily one or two students can disrupt the flow of learning, but they also know when to go with the flow, when to take a stand, and how to quell minor disturbances without further distracting others.

A friend of mine, a policeman, describes one challenge of his job: "You can look for trouble or you can look away." Like policemen, teachers must know when to do which. Some occasions are entirely predictable; others catch us off guard. Often, we must make decisions on the fly. Great teachers have learned from experience which issues demand immediate attention and which will wait for a more teachable moment.

Hey, Pretzel Face!

If the most mature student in your school is walking down the hallway and another student yells an insulting comment, what happens next?

"Hey, pretzel face!" What does the mature student do? Most likely, shrug off the taunt, possibly even with a smile. On the other hand, an immature student may feel compelled to respond in kind, or even escalate the incident to a confrontation.

Of course, I'm not suggesting that I would ignore a student who called me "pretzel face." But I am suggesting that great teachers don't automatically react every time a student steps a little out of line. We've all known teachers whose buttons are easily pushed, and we've seen how quickly students identify these teachers and their entertainment value!

If three kids in a class are talking inappropriately, the teacher might say something like, "Folks, let's quiet down." The students respond, but not all in the same way. One of the students says, "Sorry," and gets quiet. (This student has the repairing skills we talked about in Chapter 9.) One student just goes silent and looks down. The third retorts, "We weren't the only ones talking!" At this point, the teacher has a choice. One teacher might snipe back—"But you were the ones I was talking to!"—and escalate the skirmish into a battle of wills; another might ignore the remark and let the confrontation subside. Effective teachers model self-control; their classroom management is grounded in their ability to manage their own behavior.

Great teachers have the ability to ignore—but this doesn't mean that they ignore their students. Paradoxically, the students who misbehave often do so simply because they want attention. In some cases, it doesn't seem to matter whether that attention is negative or positive. But great teachers know how to give their students the attention they need, right from the start. Misbehavior doesn't spiral out of control in their classrooms, because they stay ahead of the curve.

Ignoring Minor Errors

In a study examining differences between more effective and less effective school leaders, Doug Fiore (1999) determined that one significant variation is that the very best leaders ignore minor errors. The less effective the principal, the greater the likelihood that teachers will describe that leader's comments as consistently negative. If principals do harp on minor errors, the faculty shies away from contact or interaction with them. For the sake of our own self-worth, we tend to stay away from someone who regularly points out our mistakes. (After all, who among us really welcomes the sort of faultfinding that is presented in the guise of "constructive criticism"?)

A friend of mine is a truly outstanding principal. When a new superintendent arrived in his district, my friend was eager for him to visit his school. His faculty and staff had done some outstanding things and he was proud to have others see them.

Soon, the superintendent did come to visit. After a couple of hours dropping into classrooms, he sat down in the principal's office. He asked the name of the teacher who had the end room in the first hallway. That was good news to the principal, because it was Mr. Martin, a second-year teacher and one of his best. The principal happily related what innovative ideas Mr. Martin had brought to the building and what a great role model he was for the students.

However, the superintendent then said that the reason he asked was that Mr. Martin had been using the overhead projector—and a couple of times, for a second or two, his hand obscured the screen. Yikes! Talk about nitpicking!

We can all imagine how this felt to the principal. With so many wonderful things going on, the district leader's first visit to the school was summed up in the most trivial of criticisms. Not only was it hurtful, but also it took away any incentive to welcome the superintendent for another visit. And more than that, it put a damper on the principal's efforts. He is still effective in his school, but he has pulled back; his accomplishments no longer have district-wide impact.

The superintendent in this situation had a choice. He could have ignored the thumb obscuring the overhead and everything would have been fine. The relationship between the two administrators would have had a chance to grow. Instead, he focused on something irrelevant and trivial, permanently stunting their relationship.

How do we apply this information as teachers? We are often our own worst critic. Although we may think that when others criticize us we try harder, at some point, when it happens too frequently, we are likely to quit. Just as with our own children, if we say, 'no' too often, their response becomes to tune us out completely. For example, if we want a student to create writing that has passion and voice, we might have to tolerate a missed comma periodically so they will be willing to break new ground in their writing development. If we continually nitpick at a child's writing, they will eventually only use simple words they know how to spell in very short sentences in order to avoid the wrath of the red pen. This is even more true with the most talented students.

Handling the High Achievers

High achievers hold themselves to lofty standards. They expect to succeed at everything they do and work exceedingly hard to do so. That is one reason they are so good.

When high achievers have their shortcomings pointed out by someone else, they emotionally deflate. They are used to expecting tremendous things of themselves and they hate to let others down. High achievers put so much of themselves into what they do that any criticism, no matter how minor, can become a personal affront. Furthermore, if our assessment of their work does nothing but point out minor flaws in their achievements, they may take fewer risks the next time around.

If you ask high achievers about their own performance, they will be much more critical than you would ever dream of being. I remember observing a wonderful lesson—one of those magic moments in the classroom. In the post-observation conference, I opened the discussion by asking the teacher how she thought the class went. She spent several minutes picking apart a magnificent lesson! I finally interrupted her to focus on all the positive things I had observed. My praise enhanced our relationship; I was always welcome to observe in her classroom. She never stopped being judgmental of herself, but that is part of what made her special.

Students who are high achievers respond the same way. No matter how much we push them, they are much harder on themselves. They don't want to settle for less than their best; they don't want to be told that a first draft is "fine," even though it might be far better than another student's third revision. On the other hand, they don't want to be ignored. Great teachers understand how to give these students the kind of attention that keeps them moving forward under their own steam.

A great teacher resembles the master chef who can keep a busy kitchen cooking along in the midst of what looks like chaos to the uninformed. The great teacher has the ability to ignore trivial disturbances and the ability to respond to inappropriate behavior without escalating the situation. The great teacher has the ability to pay attention to students, to recognize and praise their achievements, and the ability to overlook minor errors. It's a fast-paced and delicate balancing act; the great teacher has mastered this essential skill.

11
Random
or Plandom?

One hallmark of great teachers is that in their classrooms, very little happens at random. Great teachers have a plan and purpose for everything they do. If things don't work out the way they had envisioned, they reflect on what they could have done differently and adjust their plans accordingly.

In contrast, their less effective colleagues seem to move through their days by the roll of the dice. In some ways, it almost seems as if they don't want to have a plan; they don't want to take responsibility for what happens. If things don't work out as well as they had hoped, they look for something or someone else to blame. Here are some examples.

Why Does Jimmy Always Pick Billy?

I can remember hearing one teacher exclaim, "Every time I have group work, Jimmy and Billy pick each other as partners—and they never get any work done!" Why do Jimmy and Billy always end up as partners? The teacher allows it to happen. Time and again, the outcome is the same; time and again, the teacher chooses not to intervene. It's easier to complain about the results than to plan for a different course of events.

A great teacher may allow students to choose their own work partners. The first time, Jimmy and Billy may choose each other and accomplish little. But this teacher, reflecting on the outcome, will do something differently. Perhaps students will pick a partner's name from a bucket; in that case, the teacher can manipulate the buckets so Jimmy and Billy are sure to work with new partners. Or students may be paired up alphabetically, or simply instructed to choose a partner they haven't worked with before. Whatever the plan, the great teacher has taken responsibility.

The All-school Assembly

Several times a year, most schools gather their students in the gymnasium or auditorium for a school assembly. Now, suppose an observer from another planet could detect rays—we'll call them "teacher-rays" or "T-rays"—between each cluster of students and the teacher responsible for them. I predict that the rays emanating from the great teachers would show a typical and distinctive pattern.

When the best teachers take their students to an assembly, what do they do? They sit by their students—and not just any students, but the students who are most likely to disrupt. The best teachers aren't rude to these students, but they make their presence felt. Their T-rays send a message that is pleasant but firm; the students—perhaps to their own amazement—are on their best behavior.

Now, contrast that to the less effective teachers. Our extra-terrestrial observer is likely to see them sitting with other teachers, leaning against the wall, or even leaving the room. If they do sit with students, they choose their own comfort zone. As a result, their T-rays must travel farther to reach the students most likely to cause a commotion. These teachers have to boost their T-rays with glares, and still some of their charges behave poorly. Then the teachers can complain, "See what I have to put up with!" Their focus is on the behavior of others rather than on their own. They haven't learned the power of taking responsibility.

The Faculty Meeting

I have always been amazed at how many faculty meetings harbor a cluster of negative teachers—the Cynics Club—who sit together in the back and near the door. I am also astonished that principals feel comfortable leading a group like that. I never had the ability to manage a faculty meeting with a group of inattentive or disrespectful people in the back of the room. After a time, I learned to take matters into my own hands. I developed a plan.

Instead of allowing the Cynics Club to retain its traditional seats, I would get rid of every extra chair and then switch the back of the room to the front. When the yawners and grumblers drifted into the meeting late (as usual), the only seats left open were in the front row. Additionally, I would have my assistant principal sit next to the Great High Cynic—the most negative staff member in the school—not in an intimidating way, but very politely. Nevertheless, it had the effect of making that person more uncomfortable, less vocal, and less likely to spread an atmosphere of negativity through the room. By taking responsibility, I managed to change the dynamics of the meeting. This same approach applies in the classroom.

Great teachers intentionally arrange, rearrange, alter, and adjust the structures that frame their teaching. Their classroom setup, their instructional approaches, their time management—all are carefully planned to promote a productive learning environment. If two students cannot sit by each other peaceably, they no longer sit by each other. If one student tends to be disruptive, the teacher takes steps to minimize that student's impact on others in the room. If a class spirals into rowdiness by the end of the day, the schedule of activities makes room for them to let off steam appropriately.

These alterations do not involve a power struggle. They may seem random, but they have a definite underlying intent. There is no advantage to challenging and escalating the events that get in the way of learning. The teacher who needs to prove, over and over, who is in charge of the classroom is wasting precious energy on a losing battle. Great teachers do not try to prove who is in charge in their classrooms; everyone knows.

12

Base
Every Decision
on the Best People

We may have been taught to "teach to the middle," where the majority of the students cluster. However, as long as we teach to the middle, that is where the majority of our students will remain. Great teachers take a different approach. Great teachers aim high. Great teachers make decisions following three simple guidelines:

1. What is the purpose?
2. Will this actually accomplish the purpose?
3. What will the best people think?

The first rule seems very straightforward—but it's easy to get sidetracked. One way of reflecting on our teaching practices is to look at *why we do what we do.* Too often, however, we frame this exploration in the wrong way. Instead of asking *what is the purpose,* we settle for *what is the reason?*

Take, for example, the question of why we choose a particular homework assignment. Why assign page 62? Well, the *reason* might be that page 62 follows page 61, or that we assigned 62 last year. Why ask students to solve 25 math problems? The *reason* might be that there are 25 problems on the page, or that 25 divides evenly into 100%. But if we ask *what is the purpose,* we may end up heading in a more productive direction.

Another example might be "trade and grade"—the long-familiar practice of having students swap papers and mark each other's answers. (In the olden days, we might even have tallied the grades by asking each student to call out the result.) Why do we do this? Well, the *reason* makes sense—it's convenient for the teacher. But if we follow the model of great teachers and ask *what is the purpose,* we may decide to use class time far differently.

Shoplifters Will Be Prosecuted!

My wife and I love to go antique shopping. All too often, we see signs like this one:

Shoplifters <u>Will</u> Be Prosecuted!

We always chuckle at the added emphasis of capitalizing every word, and even underlining the word *will*. We picture the light-fingered antique buff thinking, "I was going to steal from this store, but they underlined the word *will*!"

What is the purpose of the sign? Is it to keep the honest shoppers honest? If that were the case, we'd all lapse into shoplifting in the stores that don't post such signs. Will the sign keep shoplifters from shoplifting? They already know it's against the law.

My wife and I always wonder whether these signs do any good. In fact, we have a hunch that they might actually do harm. Imagine browsing through a store. Every time you turn a corner, you encounter another sign:

Shoplifters Will Be Prosecuted!
We Are Watching You!
For the Arrest and Conviction of a Shoplifter…

Does this make you feel more comfortable, or less? A raft of aggressive anti-shoplifting signs may make the honest shoppers so uncomfortable that they change their behavior and shop somewhere else. Meanwhile, the hard-core shoplifters disregard the signs—or even take them as a challenge.

What has happened here? The store owners have a purpose in mind, but they haven't thought through the question, *will this actually accomplish the purpose?* The store owners have focused on the shoplifters and ignored their "best people"—their customers. Wouldn't they be better off in the long run with a store full of customers?

This Means You!

As a principal, I often felt very much like a business manager, responsible for making decisions, setting policies, getting things done. Inevitably, some employees gripe and complain, others drag their feet, and the top performers embrace change. The challenge for the manager is to focus on the ones who do their jobs well.

As teachers, you have no doubt found yourself on the receiving end of a principal's decisions and directives. In my book *Dealing With Difficult Teachers* (1999), I gave the example of the sign above the copy machine: "Limit: 20 Copies!" The purpose, of course, is to keep certain people from overusing the copier. But what happens? Well, those who usually follow the rules take the message to heart. Remembering one occasion seven years ago when they made 23 copies, they wonder if they should reimburse the school. On the other hand, the folks who abuse the copy machine already know they shouldn't—but they do it anyway. They'll just ignore our sign, or add a string of zeros behind the 20, or take it down and make 28 copies of it!

It's a mistake to focus on the least effective people, issuing broad directives because of one or two miscreants. At best, we make our top performers feel guilty; at worst, we insult them. They think, "Why are you talking to me about this? Why don't you talk to them?" And they're right.

As teachers, you face the same challenge within your classrooms. Think of the situation when term paper deadlines approach. Blanket statements like "You all aren't turning in your rough drafts on time!" not only allow laggards to hide in anonymity, but also make your best students worry—Did they forget to turn in their draft? Did you misplace their work?—or even slack off. What was the point of staying up late to finish that draft, if they're only going to get "yelled at" along with the rest?

What Will My Best Students Think?

Before making any decision or attempting to bring about any change, effective educators ask themselves one central question: *What will the best people think?* This does not mean that effective educators do not consider views from anyone else; but they *always* consider what the best people will think.

In a study of more effective and less effective middle school principals (Whitaker 1993), I found three critical hall-

marks of the best principals. One was that they routinely con-
sulted informal teacher leaders for input before they ever
made a decision. Why? Well, ask yourself these two questions:

- If the best teachers don't think something is a
  good idea, what are the chances that the rest of the
  faculty will accept it?
- If the best teachers don't think something is a
  good idea, what are the chances that it is a good
  idea?

As a principal, I regularly bounced ideas off a handful of
my key staff members before I made a decision. Their acceptance was an important step toward implementation of any
change.

You can take the same approach with your students. Asking yourself *what will the best students think?* can help you manage your classroom like a well-run business.

One easily remembered standard for classroom management is that we always treat our students as if their parents
were in the room. Another is that we treat every student with
the best students in mind—not necessarily the ones with the
best grades, but the nicest, most caring, most well
rounded—the students who are most welcome in our classrooms. Our best students do want misbehavior addressed, but
never in a humiliating way. They do want us to deal with the
students who disrupt learning, but they want us to do it
respectfully.

I recently visited a school where an unidentified student
had been writing on the stalls in the boys' restroom. After
their efforts to apprehend the culprit failed, the principals re-
moved the doors from the stalls. The purpose was to discour-
age graffiti—and the principals may have thought removing
the doors would accomplish this purpose. But their response
focused on the perpetrator and ignored the feelings of all the
other students whose privacy was invaded. If they had asked
the third question—*What will the best people think?*—they
might have come up with a better approach.

My Best Students "Will Be Fine" No Matter What

One of the ideas that I hear regularly from school principals is that they focus on their average or poor teachers because their best teachers "will be fine anyhow." Well, I agree that the best teachers will be fine if you ignore them—but if your best teachers are only fine, they are no longer great.

Sure, these highly talented individuals will be fine on their own. The atmosphere in their classrooms will remain positive; they will always treat their students with dignity and their colleagues with respect. But when the principal's focus shifts away from what the superstars need most, they begin to pull back. It's as if they close their door to the school—not physically, but emotionally. Principals need the best teachers to influence their grade level, their team, their department, and the entire school. Schools can't afford to drain away the dedication of the most valuable staff members by focusing on the others.

The same principle applies to our best students. If we teach to the middle, we sell our best students short. The atmosphere in a well-run classroom is charged with positive energy; every student is engaged. If our top students can coast along in neutral, the entire class loses momentum. Great teachers find a way to keep every student in gear and moving forward. We cannot afford for our best students to be "fine anyhow." They deserve much more than that.

The Teacher's Pet

It's important not to put any student in the position of being seen as the teacher's pet. It's fine to consider what the best people will think, but we must use discretion in asking for input and feedback. If other students perceive the relationship as favoritism, they may lose respect for, and even resent, the ones singled out for special treatment.

This concept of centering on the best people may seem new and unfamiliar, yet it is one of the crucial differences between the best educators and the rest. Nurture the superstar students you have, and work to cultivate others. Keep your best, most well rounded students at the forefront when you make decisions. Your classes will be better off—and your job will be more enjoyable!

13

In Every Situation, Ask Who Is Most Comfortable and Who Is Least Comfortable

All educators face the challenge of balancing rules and guidelines with those times when we need to make exceptions. This is especially true when it comes to behavior expectations for students. We can be concise, be clear, and communicate—but situations still arise when tough decisions are much more in shades of gray than we wish.

Likewise, all teachers establish internal ground rules that reflect our core belief systems, even though it seems that at least some of the time other influences tread on them. This chapter presents one internal standard that supports effective practices: When making decisions, ask *who is most comfortable and who is least comfortable in this situation?* This goes along with the guideline from Chapter 12: *Make every decision based on the best people.*

Treat Everyone As If They Were Good

A friend of mine has made a good living—in fact, a fortune—by buying apartment buildings, fixing them up, and renting them out. Any time someone I know becomes successful doing something I could probably do, I'm intrigued to learn more about it. One night I asked what he does if he purchases a building with undesirable tenants living in one of the apartments. His response struck a chord: "If there are tenants I would rather not have, I just remodel their apartment. They're not used to living in a nice place, so they either start behaving as if they deserve to stay there or they become so uncomfortable that they move out."

The same phenomenon occurs in our schools: When people become uncomfortable, they change. As a principal, I took care to make this work for me. I wanted the ones who were uncomfortable to change in a positive direction; I didn't want to create an uncomfortable situation for my best teachers. Let's look at an example involving a faculty meeting.

If Mr. Negativity dominates the meeting with carping criticism, the best teachers will be uncomfortable. The less positive faculty members may actually enjoy it. If I lose my cool and react unprofessionally, my best teachers become even more uncomfortable and distance themselves. But what if I handle the situation with aplomb? I might say, "I think that is a point worth pursuing. Let's talk about it later this week. I'm usually here by 6:30; pick a morning that works for you." Mr. Negativity has lost his audience (and will have to get up early if he wants to keep griping). The most positive staff members will gratefully align themselves on my side.

We can apply the same principle to working with parents. I recently saw a memo sent home with all 800 students in a school. The note said:

Dear Parents,

You MUST pick your child up promptly any time we have an away field trip and the field trip buses return after the regular buses have left! *If you do not,* your child could be placed in after-school daycare and you could be charged up to $2.00 an hour.

Now ask yourself: Out of 800 families, how many were that note actually written for? Probably three or four—ironically, the three or four least likely to read the note. This school has insulted some 795 families because of a small minority of others. What's more, these three or four already knew they were supposed to pick up their children; they just didn't do it. The note addressed to the entire population actually allows them to be more comfortable. They can think to themselves, "There must be lots of us who don't pick up our children on time."

On the other hand, the rest of the folks are wondering, "What are you talking to me for?" The decision to send a note to everyone makes all the responsible parents uncomfortable in the hope of reaching a few. A more effective approach would be to call the small number of negligent parents—making *them* uncomfortable.

As a rule, I'm not a big fan of sending out notes. But if you feel that some kind of general reminder is necessary, focus on the positive families and treat everyone as if they were good. A note could read:

> Dear Parents,
>
> Thank you for your support in picking up your child promptly any time we have an away field trip and the field trip buses return after the regular buses have left. This enables us to provide more educational opportunities for our students and provides a safer environment for all the young people in our schools. Thank you for your efforts.

This message is just as effective a reminder to the small number of parents who were not there to pick up their children. The difference is that the note reinforces the good behavior; it makes the prompt parents more comfortable and the late ones uncomfortable.

This approach can guide decisions in many areas. Think of the teacher who spends the first day with a finger-pointing lecture about the rules. Which students are most uncomfortable? The ones who don't need a host of rules to keep them in line. What are the others doing? Plotting!

Think of the teacher who punishes an entire class because of a few students' behavior. Maybe the misbehaving students feel some level of discomfort, but certainly the most responsible students are upset and have much less respect for the teacher. Teachers who ask themselves, "How will my best students feel as a result of my decision?" will probably take a different approach to discipline.

If a teacher uses a cutting remark to stop misbehavior, the student it was directed at may temporarily fall in line. But at what cost? The well-behaved students are uncomfortable; they are not used to hearing people talk like that. The students whom teachers are most tempted to yell at are probably quite used to it. However, the other students lose respect for a teacher who relies on putdowns or tirades.

A teacher considering whether to have students grade each other's papers and call out the grades for the teacher to record them might ask, "Who is most comfortable in this situation?" The students with low grades surely aren't comfortable; often, even those with high grades would rather not have attention called to their performance. This convenient shortcut benefits only the teacher.

If all the classes in the school are in session and the two rowdiest troublemakers in the school are walking down the hall, what do teachers say to them? Most likely things like, "Where are you supposed to be?" "Whose class are you out of?" "Didn't that bell mean anything to you?" We treat them as if they're bound to be up to no good.

But what if it's the future valedictorian and salutatorian in the hallway? They're greeted with a friendly smile. "Hi, how's your day going?" Our natural tendency is to treat them as if they were good. Now, is there a way we can accomplish what we want by treating both groups the same—as if they were good?

Yes, there is. We could greet all students with, "Hi. Can I help you?" Doesn't that get the same information from the troublemakers as the other approach? But if they are not doing anything wrong, we have not escalated the situation; and the other two students would not see it as an insult.

Remember the antique-store customers and the shoplifters. Couldn't we handle both of them the same way? Do customers mind if a smiling clerk asks, "Can I help you?" And wouldn't that prevent shoplifting just as much as snapping in an accusatory tone, "What are you doing over there?" The difference is that we have not set up a scenario where someone needs to get back at someone else. We have treated everyone as if they were good.

Uncomfortable Feelings Make People Change—One Way or Another

If a teacher argues with a belligerent parent, who feels uncomfortable? Not the parent; hostile parents love to argue. It's their niche. That's one good reason never to argue with difficult people—they have a lot more practice at it! However, another reason is that part of our job as teachers is to teach people appropriate ways to behave, not just help them refine the inappropriate skills they already have in abundance.

No, it's the teacher who argues with a parent who feels uncomfortable and is likely to avoid the parent. The parent actually feels empowered—free to go tell everyone how the teacher acted, what was said, and how the argument ended. That parent will come back to the school ready for battle.

Reflect on the example—"Limit: 20 Copies!"—discussed in the last chapter. This approach does make some people uncomfortable—the ones who hold themselves to high standards. The high achievers will feel affronted, and they will behave differently; they will be less enthusiastic about work and move away from the heart of the school.

On the other hand, this generalized approach has little or no impact on the people for whom it was intended. They already have managed to rationalize why they deserve to ignore the rules. If anything, now they spend even more time thinking about how to get away with something.

If applied consistently, the question "Who is most comfortable and who is least comfortable?" can bring clarity to our decision-making. We are not painting on a blank canvas; we have outlines to follow. We may decide to do something that will make the least effective people uncomfortable, but at the very least, our decisions will not make our best people uncomfortable.

Effective educators find that this ground rule—make the people who do the right thing feel comfortable—works for them too. They feel more comfortable with their decision-making!

Pay for Performance

Sometimes understanding situations that we are in ourselves can help us sort out what approaches may be appropriate with others. I now work as professor at a university. Universities sometimes follow an interesting dynamic. They often take a different approach to managerial and structural functions than most other organizations.

One trend in higher education is called "Pay for Performance." At our university, raises for faculty members are established by peer review. It's as if all of the teachers in a school voted on individual salary increases for teachers.

As you can imagine, this is a controversial process. Job performance at a university is nearly impossible to quantify. Feelings get hurt, emotions run high, and relations become strained. After the first year, a confidential survey was conducted to determine what the faculty thought about the program. I happened to run into the university president—a man I hold in high regard—just after he received the results. He was very interested in reviewing the feedback on this innovative program.

I agreed with the president that the information could be valuable. However, I added that the perspectives of the entire faculty were not the decisive factor. He asked what I meant. I said that he should identify the thirty-three percent of the faculty whom he hoped would feel rewarded by pay for performance. If his very best employees felt reinforced, then the perspectives of the others might be helpful. But if they did not, then the program was not worthwhile—no matter what the others thought.

As it happened, the survey showed that about one third liked the program, one third were neutral, and one third did not like it. Well, it sure depends which third thought what, doesn't it? If the "worst" third of the faculty is uncomfortable with the program, there may be reason to consider making it permanent. But even if only five percent of the faculty disapprove, if that five percent represents the cream of the crop, then it is critical to revisit the entire concept. What really matters is what the best people think.

It is always okay to gather everyone's input. But it is more important to be aware of what our best people's views are. Many students—like many adults—make decisions based on what is best for them. The best students—like the best adults—make decisions based on what is best for everyone. If we seek input from our most capable students and colleagues, we are much more likely to make the right choices.

Effective educators continually ask themselves who is most comfortable and who is least comfortable with each decision they make. When we face a challenging decision, we'll feel less alone if we ask ourselves, "What will the best people think?" And we'll feel even less alone if we go to our best people and ask them what they think.

14

What About These Darn Standardized Tests?

As a writer, speaker, and professor, I do my best to stay focused on enduring issues in our schools. I care most about staff motivation, teacher morale, school culture and climate, and student behavior. These core issues have been central to our schools—all schools—for decades and will remain essential decades from now. Likewise, I tend to stay away from the hot issue of the day (or year, or decade).

Effective teachers don't let hot-button issues shift their focus from what really matters. The best educators spend their human resources carefully, aware of the limited value of many mandates from on high. With this context as the backdrop, I'm now going to tiptoe into the shark-infested pool of standardized testing.

Without Success, Tests Become the School

If you want to hear an emotional debate, bring up politics or religion—but if you overhear teachers arguing about one of these mainstream topics and want to escalate the battle, ask them to share their views on standardized testing. Although mandated testing has been around in some states for decades, it is still evolving everywhere. The tests change, testing dates change, different grade levels are included or excluded, open-ended assessments are on the horizon. And each change in state or federal testing requirements brings another opportunity to discuss the merits of that change and of testing in general.

Like everyone else, teachers have different personal viewpoints on standardized testing. Yet, no matter what our beliefs, we must deal with the reality of standardized tests. How do we go about it?

First of all, we must move away from debating the merits of standardized testing. Strongly held personal beliefs tend to dominate that debate. We must shift our focus away from beliefs and center on behaviors. If we can agree on behaviors, we can move forward in harmony regardless of our personal feelings. Like two parents with differing beliefs on discipline, we can work toward consensus on the consistent *behaviors* that are essential for success.

If we brought together all our different constituent groups—teachers, parents, administrators, board members, students, community representatives—we might be surprised to discover how much we agree on. Here's an exercise to share with your school. Let's imagine that we ask all these people, either collectively or individually, a couple of key questions.

The first and most important question is this:

♦ *What should our schools be doing?*

I believe we will find an affirming overlap of answers. Although some may want more emphasis on math or physical education, arts or technology, our different constituent groups generally agree on what schools should be doing. We can represent this area of agreement as one big circle, shown in Figure 14-1.

Figure 14-1

*What
Schools
Should Be Doing*

Now, let's ask the same groups—again either collectively or individually—question number two:

♦ *What do standardized tests measure?*

Although there are explicit listings of most state test standards, people still have a variety of beliefs about what they actually measure. Whatever their beliefs are, let's represent them in a smaller circle, shown with the larger circle in Figure 14-2.

Figure 14-2

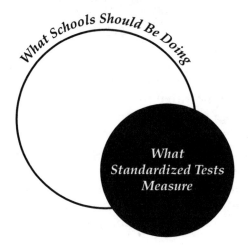

Ask your colleagues whether they feel that, on the whole, these two circles depict their personal views regarding the relationship between what schools should be doing and what standardized tests measure. Before they respond, you might note that some may think the second circle, or the overlap between the two, should be larger (or smaller). Don't get into a hairsplitting contest. Instead, ask whether they agree that the first circle is the core of your school.

Next comes the essential step: shifting the focus from views and beliefs to behaviors. No matter how we personally see the relationship between the small circle and the large circle, we as educators must achieve success within the smaller circle or it will become our big circle (Figure 14-3)—and no one in a school wants that.

Figure 14-3

Even the teacher who least believes in standardized test-ing now has an incentive to work toward student success in this area. We can now center on the same behaviors, working toward the same goal *regardless of our beliefs*. We can maintain our personal beliefs about the merits of testing while we move our school toward success.

Standardized tests measure only a part of what schools should be doing. Effective teachers focus on the behaviors that lead to success, not the beliefs that stand in the way of it. Effec-tive teachers don't let standardized tests take over the entire class.

Raise Those Test Scores!

Many of us have attended meetings where an administra-tor ranted and raved about the need to improve our school's scores on standardized state tests. (The all-too-familiar chant—"Raise those test scores!"—reminds me of a track coach yelling, "Run faster!" If we want our athletes to run faster, we need to teach them how. The same applies to raising test scores.)

In any case, how we respond to such tirades during that meeting is one thing; more critical is what we do—how we fil-ter events—afterwards. If someone asks, "How was the meet-ing?" we can respond, "Fine." (Or even, "Not too bad, thanks.") Of course, we'll continue our efforts to increase student achievement—but at the same time, we can avoid spreading our own disgruntlement to others.

Even though standardized testing is one of the most controversial topics we deal with, some teachers never allow their personal views to affect discussions they might have with student, parents, or even peers. Others consistently choose to fan the flames of controversy. We each make our decisions on what to share and what to leave out.

Effective Teachers Keep Testing in Perspective

In a study of schools that exceeded expectations on standardized tests (Turner 2002), the perspectives of the educators were very refreshing. The teachers and principals in those schools did not believe in the value of testing more than others; they just understood the importance of test results to others. They were fully aware that success on standardized tests brought them greater autonomy to do what they believed was best for students. These educators also understood how the tests and state standards could provide a powerful backdrop for improving and aligning curriculum. Before state-mandated testing, for many teachers the textbook was their curriculum. The state standards forced educators to shift the focus to what our curriculum was and helped us center on the real issue of student learning.

However, the teachers and principals in the more effective schools in the study described student achievement in a much broader sense than did educators whose schools underachieved on standardized tests. No matter what the socioeconomic background, schools that performed poorly defined student achievement only in terms of test scores. Effective principals (whose schools had equally diverse clientele) and their teachers mentioned test scores, but they also listed student social skills, self worth, behavior, responsibility, involvement in school, and other such characteristics as important components of student achievement.

The more effective educators were also aware of the risk of making state standards the center of the school. If your school's core rests on state standards, then you had better hope that the standards never change, because if they do, you have lost the core of your classroom and of your school. Instead, every decision should rest on doing what is best for students. Then when new mandates and programs come into play, you can examine how they fit into what you are already doing that is best for the students.

So, You Want to Improve Your Reading Scores?

Last year, a middle school that I had worked with before asked me to help improve its students' scores on state testing. Ordinarily, I turn down such requests, not because of a lack of experience in this area—as a principal, I worked in schools that achieved tremendous gains in standardized test scores—but because I prefer to focus on more pressing issues. However, because I had worked with this school on other occasions, I agreed to assist them.

But first, I asked to meet with their faculty. At that meeting, I asked the teachers one question: "Are you so interested in improving your students' reading abilities that you are willing to change what you do in your classroom—or do you want to raise their test scores *so that you don't have to change* what you do in your classroom?"

That is really the essence of education. What determines what happens in my classroom—the syllabus, or the students? Do I hold up the standards at the finish line and watch the students make their way down the track as best they can—or am I at their sides, helping them to develop the skills they need? Great teachers know the difference.

15

Make It Cool
to Care

Effective teachers have a strong core of beliefs—principles that guide their decisions, touchstones that help them distinguish right from wrong, goals that define their vision for the school year. I would like to share the core beliefs I followed in my years as a teacher and a principal. I realize that these are personal; each of you must have your own core of beliefs. I outline my beliefs here for three reasons. One is to acquaint you with their simplicity. Two is to aid in understanding that the clearer our beliefs are, the more we can keep working toward them. And three illustrates how these core beliefs frame the way we work in classrooms and schools.

Make It Cool to Care

My central goal was incredibly simple and incredibly complex. I wanted it to be "cool to care" in my room and in my school. I wanted everyone—every student, every teacher, each staff member, all the parents—to think it was cool to care. Ironically, I don't think I ever shared this goal with anyone—maybe because it sounded so simple, maybe because it might be scoffed at, and maybe to improve its chance of becoming reality. Chanting "Be drug free, you and me" during Red Ribbon Week may or may not make a difference, but I am pretty sure that when kids reach a certain age, its value diminishes. I felt the same about advertising my goal.

In this book, we have occasionally referred to trends in education. Some have had positive and lasting effects; others seem silly in hindsight. I regularly receive calls from schools and districts asking me to help them implement a program or reach a goal. Often, this undertaking relates to the latest trend or mandate. Whether I agree or not, I want the educators to understand that getting a faculty to go along with a particular undertaking has limited value. Rather, the key is to develop and establish a school-wide environment that supports everyone's effort to do what is right. If we create an environment where each person does what is best for the students and for the school, we will seldom make a wrong decision. Getting people to do the current thing is fine. Getting people to do the right thing is essential.

The best teachers are able to achieve this in their classrooms. The students care, and they care deeply. They care about learning, they care about the teacher, and they care about each other. Once it is cool to care, anything becomes possible. All the behaviors we have described in this book lead to this. Treating everyone with respect and dignity; always taking a positive approach; always modeling how to treat others; understanding that what matters is people, not programs; making every decision based on the best people—each of these helps create an environment where it is cool to care. If two people both make every decision on what is best for students, even if they don't agree, they will both be right.

Once we create an environment where it is cool to care, there are no wrong decisions. People who make the extra effort are valued. Whining is worthless; caring is keen. Think about the very best teachers in your school. If they want to, they can make any new program work. No matter what the new standards are, they can help all their students meet them. The real challenge, and the real accomplishment, is to get all the students to care about what happens in the classroom. Once we achieve that, anything is possible. Until we achieve that, any obstacle can seem insurmountable.

The Great Teacher

In Chapter 1, I described my interest in understanding what great teachers do differently. The first time this struck me was during an informal visit in the classroom of my best teacher, Mrs. Heart. I watched as Darin approached her desk—Darin, a rough, tough, tattooed discipline problem who easily intimidated the other students (and many of the teachers, and maybe the principal!). Making no effort to keep the other students from hearing him, Darin said, "Mrs. Heart, I was working on my poetry last night and I had a hard time with some of the words in the third verse. I was wondering if I could get your help on..." My jaw must have hit the floor.

Believe me, Darin was not a fan of poetry. Darin was a fan of Mrs. Heart. She had made it cool to care about whatever was happening in class. No matter what the focus, the students shared that focus. When the state set new standards, I never worried about Mrs. Heart. She could get the students interested in whatever the state issue was, but she never lost sight of the big picture. Mrs. Heart wasn't preparing her students for the state test. Mrs. Heart was preparing her students for life. This is what teaching is all about. Getting along with others, treating everyone with respect, doing your best—that was Mrs. Heart. She made it cool to care.

If we can raise every teacher to Mrs. Heart's level, or even close to that, we have something special. Even if teachers are just trying to get there, that is wonderful. You see, if you want to be like Mrs. Heart, then you think it is cool to care.

Merry Christmas, Everyone!

One year the junior high school where I was principal decided to adopt a partner school—a preschool whose students had multiple handicaps, including severe disabilities. I was very proud of our students. They were pen pals to the youngsters, sent them cards on their birthdays, and hosted monthly theme parties.

As the holiday season approached, our students decided to do something special for their adoptees. They decided to raise money to buy each one a hat, mittens, and a sweatshirt with our school logo emblazoned across the front. The students came up with the idea of holding a half-hour carnival during our advisory time each morning for one week. Each day, one fifth of the homerooms would host the carnival and the other students would attend. Each group thought of different booths—ring toss games, root beer floats for a quarter, jars of candy to guess the number of pieces, even raffles to throw pies at the *assistant* principal (not me).

All the booths were inexpensive; our goal was to have each homeroom raise just $10. Well, the carnival was an unqualified success. Even the homerooms with resistant teachers who took a minimal role reached the $10 goal. We then pooled the money and bought the mittens, hats, and school sweatshirts.

Students in art classes made holiday cards for the preschoolers. Home Economics classes baked cookies. All the advisories wrapped presents. Then came the day of the big party at the preschool. I had each homeroom teacher "randomly" select one student to help. (The faculty knew that in such situations, "random" meant the student who would benefit most.) The band played, the choir sang, the orchestra performed, and the drama students did holiday skits. I even chose a student to wear my personal Santa Claus suit and play St. Nick at the festivities. We caught the entire party on video—the severely handicapped students sitting on Santa's lap (or as close as they could); everyone enjoying the music; our students comfortably and fearlessly holding and entertaining the preschoolers; excited children opening their presents. It was something special.

Two days later, as part of our traditional all-school holiday assembly, we wheeled out several large-screen televisions and played the tape of the party. Everyone got to see the love and joy that we brought into these youngsters' lives. They got to see the special children they had "adopted" look with amazement into Santa's eyes. Tears came easily when our students saw the video of these very challenged children hugging their classmates. By the time the tape ended, there were few dry eyes in the auditorium. And this was a group of junior high students!

Then, after the tape was over, the curtains opened on stage. There were all our very special preschool friends, in their matching sweatshirts with our school name and mascot, singing carols to us. No one in that room will ever forget it. You see, that is school.

We didn't have any fights in school the rest of the week; no one was even referred to the office. And we never had a problem with students teasing any of their own handicapped peers who attended our junior high. The impact on the students was dramatic, but even more significant was the effect on our least positive staff members. After that, whenever we did something as a school, all the advisory teachers willingly rolled up their sleeves and joined in. Once it becomes cool to care, there are no limits to what can be accomplished.

Who Are the Legends?

In great schools, the teachers tell stories about what other teachers have accomplished with students. The heroes are not the contract-negotiating team, but those who have the greatest impact on the students. In one school I visited, the legendary figures were teachers who had students move in with them, and staff members who worked with children late into the night.

Some folks keep alive the legend of teachers who knock a student down with a single sarcastic comment; others revere those who pick the students up. Every educator needs to know which teachers are the legends. Effective leaders work to make sure the ones on the pedestal are the best ones. Cultivating this environment is essential to developing a great school.

I recently worked with a school where unprofessional attitudes and behaviors were common. Faculty members put students down and thought that failing a student showed how good the teacher was. In trying to change this culture, I met with eight of the top teachers in the school and shared my concerns about the underlying attitude and tone. They nodded in agreement but were not sure what to do about it.

Eventually, one teacher asked if they should stand up to their negative peers. In response, I told them what one outstanding teacher did in a similar situation. At a dysfunctional school where I was the new principal, many on the staff habitually made sarcastic and derogatory remarks—not gentle teasing, but much more negative and usually hurtful. When this happened, one particular teacher's response stood out in my eyes. When her colleagues used inappropriate and hurtful humor, she didn't confront them—she simply didn't laugh.

"And that is what I need you to do too," I told the group of concerned teachers. "Just do what is right, no matter what others do around you." That is what the great teachers do. They do what is right no matter what else is going on.

Touch the Heart, Then Teach the Child

We are often tempted to use logic as a motivator. "This quiz is worth ten points." "If everyone talks at once, nobody can hear." "Sign up for the honors section—it will look good on your transcript." There is nothing wrong with that at times. But we must realize that emotions play a part too. Year after year, we ask students to venture into the strange territory of new information, new skills. We try to link the new material to familiar ground: "Fractions are like dividing a pizza into equal pieces—the remainder is like the cookies left on the plate when each child at the party gets two." But the wobbly bridge between the familiar and the new can be scary. Many students and adults do not try because they are afraid—maybe of failure, maybe of humiliation. Who knows? Maybe they do not even know. To overcome this obstacle, we have to rely on emotion ourselves.

Think about adults who are afraid of flying. We can present all sorts of facts about how flying is safer than driving, and it probably won't make any difference. They may even agree with us about the facts. They don't have a logical reason for staying on the ground; they are afraid. However, if an emergency arises and they need to be with a faraway family member quickly, they might readily decide to fly anyway. Their emotions overcome their irrational fear.

We can use the same approach when we are hoping to reach our students. When a teacher's sensitivity to students increases, so does the opportunity to reach them. We can present logical reasons why each student should give a teacher attention and respect, but that alone will not work with many students. It is easy to convince ourselves that we can't work with one student, or several. But until we connect with them emotionally, we may never be able to connect with their minds. Great educators understand that behaviors and beliefs are tied to emotion, and they understand the power of emotion to jump-start change.

I'll give you an example. When I became principal of an eighth-grade center (adolescence at its finest!), the tone in the school was less than positive. Several teachers did not hold students in the regard that I feel is essential. This attitude carried over to their classrooms and the way they treated and interacted with students, especially students who were less than teacher-pleasers in appearance or attitude.

The only thing I could think of was to attempt to reach the emotional side of the faculty. With the help of an outstanding high school counselor, we put together a panel of students who attended our school the previous year but who had not succeeded here—not major discipline or attendance problems, just pretty nice kids, the kind who easily fall through the cracks. They don't draw attention to themselves, but they are not interested in school, not involved, not connected.

Six students agreed to be panelists at a faculty meeting. The only prepping they received was to be honest. What happened over the next hour was unbelievably emotional. The students shared that they thought none of their teachers liked them. They thought no one cared. They were not even sure some of their teachers knew their names. It was quite sad. But, then, one of my coldest staff members blurted out, "Well, maybe if you had just done your homework you would have done better. Maybe if you had tried more you would have been more successful. Maybe if you had studied more you wouldn't have flunked my class!"

What happened next was powerful. Nothing happened. No one agreed. No one chimed in. I could almost sense the other teachers moving their chairs away from him. This teacher had moved from being a negative leader on the staff to total isolation. Maybe none of my other teachers stood up to him, but one thing they did sure made me proud. None of them laughed.

Great teachers impact others in more ways than they can ever know. The legacies we build last far beyond our years. Students care about great teachers because they know great teachers care about them.

16

Clarifying
Your Core

Every teacher's experience is unique, and every classroom is different. But great teachers—no matter where or whom or what they teach—have much in common. This book has highlighted fourteen hallmarks of great teachers—their attitudes, goals, decisions, and practices. In the end, the difference lies in the core of beliefs that guide their work. In this book, I have blended findings from several studies with conclusions drawn from less formal observations and interactions. More than that, I have shared the core of what matters to me.

I hold fast to certain essential beliefs. I'm convinced that the teacher is the filter for whatever happens in a classroom. I believe that the quality of the teachers determines the quality of the school. I recognize that in any school, some programs work more successfully than others—but I'm sure that success comes from people, not programs. I insist on the importance of treating every person with respect and dignity, every single day.

On the other hand, some aspects of the day-to-day routine of school don't matter much to me. I have always worked to be punctual, but I never kept close tabs on whether teachers arrived by the official check-in time, as long as they were effective with their students.

In my first years as a teacher, the principal required us all to turn in our lesson plans each week. I diligently did so, spending extra time to write them neatly and work for continuity. I also remember that as a result, I spent less time actually planning and preparing for class.

When I became a principal, I too collected lesson plans from my teachers—for about two weeks. But on reflection, I realized that what mattered was not neat lesson plans for me, but effective lesson plans for the students. At least at first glance, there was little connection between an effective teacher and a tidy plan book. When I thought about my best teachers, I realized they must see this requirement as just another hassle. What's more, I had only asked for lesson plans because someone else did—and I hadn't chosen a good role model. Of course, I have nothing against planning for lessons, and it might be a good idea to review the lesson plans of a poorly prepared teacher. But I decided not to take time and energy away from what mattered—engaging with students effectively.

Being a teacher is an amazing profession. It is challenging, dynamic, energizing, and draining—but most of all, it is rewarding. Our impact extends far beyond anything we can imagine. We know that our students talk about us; so do our colleagues, and so do people throughout our community. We can decide what we want those conversations to be like.

Every teacher feels the pressure of outside influences. Everyone in the community has a vested interest in schooling—and everyone who ever went to school can claim to be an expert. This is not a criticism, just a fact of human nature. However, as educators we must adhere to our core values. No matter what others want us to do, we must focus on what is right for our students.

At times, being a teacher can be lonely. Though we spend our days with students, their perspective on the day is not the same as ours. Though we work in a community of colleagues, at times we have to make decisions on our own. Without a core of firmly held beliefs, it's difficult to steer a steady course. With this core, we feel secure and confident. And most importantly, so will our students.

This book does not present a cookie-cutter approach to teaching, or a narrow doorway to success. Instead it shows the framework that sustains the work of all great educators. Think of it as a blueprint. The teachers are the architects. The lessons are the foundation. The students move into the building and fill it with life and meaning.

Every teacher has an impact. Great teachers make a difference.

Fourteen Things That Matter Most

1. Great teachers never forget that it is people, not programs, that determine the quality of a school.
2. Great teachers establish clear expectations at the start of the year and follow them consistently as the year progresses.
3. When a student misbehaves, great teachers have one goal: to keep that behavior from happening again.
4. Great teachers have high expectations for students but even higher expectations for themselves.
5. Great teachers know who is the variable in the classroom: *They are.* Good teachers consistently strive to improve, and they focus on something they can control—their own performance.
6. Great teachers create a positive atmosphere in their classrooms and schools. They treat every person with respect. In particular, they understand the power of praise.
7. Great teachers consistently filter out the negatives that don't matter and share a positive attitude.
8. Great teachers work hard to keep their relationships in good repair—to avoid personal hurt and to repair any possible damage.
9. Great teachers have the ability to ignore trivial disturbances and the ability to respond to inappropriate behavior without escalating the situation.
10. Great teachers have a plan and purpose for everything they do. If things don't work out the way they had envisioned, they reflect on what they could have done differently and adjust their plans accordingly.
11. Before making any decision or attempting to bring about any change, great teachers ask themselves one central question: *What will the best people think?*

12. Great teachers continually ask themselves who is most comfortable and who is least comfortable with each decision they make. They treat everyone as if they were good.

13. Great teachers keep standardized testing in perspective; they center on the real issue of student learning.

14. Great teachers care about their students. They understand that behaviors and beliefs are tied to emotion, and they understand the power of emotion to jump-start change.

References

Bissell, B. (1992, July). *The paradoxical leader.* Paper presented at the Missouri Leadership Academy, Columbia, MO.

Ehrenberg, R. G., & Brewer, D. J. (1994). Do school and teacher characteristics matter? Evidence from high school and beyond. *Economics of Education Review, 13(1),* 1–17.

Ferguson, R. F., & Ladd, H. F. (1996). How and why money matters: An analysis of Alabama schools. In H. F. Ladd (Ed.), *Holding schools accountable. Performance-based reform in education* (pp. 265–298). Washington, DC: The Brookings Foundation.

Fiore, D. (1999). The relationship between principal effectiveness and school culture in elementary schools. (Doctoral dissertation, Indiana State University, Terre Haute, 1999.)

Goldhaber, D. D., & Brewer, D. J. (1999). Teachers licensing and student achievement. In M. Kanstoroom & C. E. Finn (Eds.), *Better teachers, better schools* (pp. 683–702). Washington, DC: The Thomas B. Fordham Foundation.

Hess, F. M. (2001). *Tear down this wall: The case for a radical overhaul of teacher certification.* Washington, DC: Progressive Policy Institute.

Kaplan, L., & Owings, W. A. (2002). The politics of teacher quality: Implications for principals. *NASSP Bulletin, 86(633),* 22–41.

Roeschlein, T. (2002). What effective middle school principals do to impact school climate. (Doctoral dissertation, Indiana State University, Terre Haute, 2002.)

Thomas, S. C. (2002, March 1). Report focuses on providing better teachers for classrooms. *St. Louis Post-Dispatch,* p. B1.

Turner, E. (2002). What effective principals do to improve instruction and increase student achievement. (Doctoral dissertation, Indiana State University, Terre Haute, 2002.)

Walsh, K. (2001). Teacher certification reconsidered: Stumbling towards quality. Baltimore, MD: Abell Foundation. Retrieved from www.abell.org/publications/detail.asp?ID=61.

Whitaker, M. E. (1997). Principal leadership behaviors in school operations and change implementations in elementary schools in relation to climate. (Doctoral dissertation, Indiana State University, Terre Haute, 1997.)

Whitaker, T. (1993). Middle school programs and climate: The principal's impact. (Doctoral dissertation, University of Missouri–Columbia, 1992.)

Whitaker, T. (1999). *Dealing with difficult teachers.* Larchmont, NY: Eye On Education.

Whitaker, T., & Fiore, D. (2001). *Dealing with difficult parents (and with parents in difficult situations).* Larchmont, NY: Eye On Education.

Whitaker, T., Whitaker, B., & Lumpa, D. (2000). *Motivating and inspiring teachers: the educational leader's guide for building staff morale.* Larchmont, NY: Eye On Education.

If you would like information about inviting Todd Whitaker to speak to your group, please contact him at t-whitaker@indstate.edu or at his web site ww.toddwhitaker.com or (812) 237–2904.

If you enjoyed this book, we recommend . . .

Great Quotes for Great Educators
Todd Whitaker and Dale Lumpa

Over 600 insightful, witty nuggets to motivate and inspire you...

...and everyone else at your school.

Teachers—display these quotes in your classrooms!

Administrators—insert them into your faculty memos and share them at staff meetings!

Why is this book *unique*?

♦ includes over 100 original quotes from internationally acclaimed speaker and educator Todd Whitaker

♦ features real quotes from real students, which echo wit and wisdom for educators

♦ each quote has a direct connection to your life as an educator

Examples of quotes in this book...

"Great teachers have high expectations for their students, but higher expectations for themselves."

Todd Whitaker

"We can never control a classroom until we control ourselves."

Todd Whitaker

2004, 150 pp. (est.) paperback 1-903556-82-9
$29.95 plus shipping and handling

Order form on page 143

Teaching Matters:
Motivating & Inspiring Yourself
Todd and Beth Whitaker

"This book makes you want to be the best teacher you can be."

Nancy Fahnstock, Godby High School
Tallahassee, Florida

Celebrate the teaching life! This book helps teachers:

♦ rekindle the excitement of the first day of school all year long

♦ approach every day in a "Thank God it is Monday" frame of mind

♦ not let negative people ruin your day

♦ fall in love with teaching all over again

Brief Contents

♦ Why You're Worth it

♦ Unexpected Happiness

♦ Could I Have a Refill Please? (Opportunities for Renewal)

♦ Celebrating Yourself

♦ Raise the Praise—Minimize the Criticize

♦ Making School Work for You

2002, 150 pp. paperback 1-930556-35-7
$24.95 plus shipping and handling

Order form on page 143

What Great Principals Do Differently:
15 Things That Matter Most
Todd Whitaker

"... affirming and uplifting, with insights into human nature and 'real people' examples..."

Edward Harris, Principal
Chetek High School, WI

What are the specific qualities and practices of great principals that elevate them above the rest? Blending school-centered studies and experience working with hundreds of administrators, Todd Whitaker reveals why these practices are effective and demonstrates how to implement each of them in your school.

Brief Contents

♦ It's People, Not Programs
♦ Who is the Variable?
♦ Hire Great Teachers
♦ Standardized Testing
♦ Focus on Behavior, Then Focus on Beliefs
♦ Base Every Decision on Your Best Teachers
♦ Make it Cool to Care
♦ Set Expectations At the Start of the Year
♦ Clarifying Your Core

2002, 130 pp. paperback 1-930556-47-0
$29.95 plus shipping and handling

Order form on page 143

Dealing with Difficult Teachers
Second Edition
Todd Whitaker

"... filled with inspirational ideas and strategies that work."

> Melanie Brock, Principal
> Westview Elementary School
> Excelsior Springs, MO

Whether you are a teacher, administrator, or fill some other role in your school, difficult teachers can make your life miserable. This book shows you how to handle staff members who:

+ gossip in the teacher's lounge.
+ consistently say "it won't work" when any new idea is suggested.
+ undermine your efforts toward school improvement.
+ negatively influence other staff members.

Added to this edition are 4 new chapters on communicating with difficult teachers.

This new section demonstrates how to:

+ eliminate negative behaviors.
+ implement effective questioning strategies.
+ apply the "The Best Teacher/Worst Teacher" test.

2002, 208 pp. paperback 1-930556-45-4
$29.95 plus shipping and handling

Order form on page 143

Motivating and Inspiring Teachers:
The Educational Leader's Guide
for Building Staff Morale
Todd Whitaker, Beth Whitaker, and Dale Lumpa

"The most appealing feature of this book is its simplicity and common sense. It is practical, useful and readable, and I recommend it."

Ron Seckler, Principal
Swope Middle School, NV

Filled with strategies to motivate and stimulate your staff, this book features simple suggestions that you can integrate into your current daily routines. It will show you how to:

♦ insert key phrases and specific actions into your day-to-day conversations, staff meetings, and written memos to stimulate peak effectiveness

♦ hire new staff and plan orientation and induction meetings to cultivate and retain loyal and motivated staff members

♦ use the "gift of time" to stimulate and reward

♦ get amazing results by not taking credit for them

♦ motivate yourself each and every day

2000, 252 pp. paperback 1-883001-99-4
$34.95 plus shipping and handling

Order form on page 143

Feeling Great!
The Educator's Guide for Eating Better, Exercising Smarter, and Feeling Your Best
Todd Whitaker and Jason Winkle

"This book will *especially* appeal to people who do not like to exercise."

Katherine Alvestad
Dowell Elementary School, MD

Educator's spend so much time taking care of others that we sometimes forget to take care of ourselves! This book will help teachers, principals, professors, and all educators find time in our busy schedules to focus on our physical self. You will learn how to:

♦ make time for exercise in your hectic daily schedule.

♦ learn how to feel your best every day.

♦ eat right even when on the go.

♦ keep your fitness momentum going all year.

♦ turn your daily routines into healthy habits.

Brief Contents

♦ Why Fitness for Educators? What's So Special About Us?

♦ But I Don't Like to Sweat

♦ Setting Realistic Goals

♦ Finding the Time and the Energy

♦ Keeping it up Through the Summer

♦ Fad or Fact? What Diets Really Work?

2002, 150 pp. paperback 1-930556-38-1
$24.95 plus shipping and handling

Order form on page 143

Dealing with Difficult Parents
(And with Parents in Difficult Situations)
Todd Whitaker & Douglas J. Fiore

"This book is an easy read with common sense appeal. The authors are not afraid to share their own vulnerability and often demonstrate a sense of humor."

Gale Hulme, Program Director
Georgia's Leadership Institute
for School Improvement

This book helps teachers, principals, and other educators develop skills in working with the most difficult parents in the most challenging situations. It shows you how to:

- ◆ avoid the "trigger" words that serve only to make bad situations worse.
- ◆ use the right words and phrases to help you develop more positive relationships with parents.
- ◆ deal with parents who accuse you of not being fair.
- ◆ build positive relationships with even the most challenging parents.

2001, 175 pp. paperback 1-930556-09-8
$29.95 plus shipping and handling

Order form on page 143

REAL Teachers,
REAL Challenges, REAL Solutions:
25 Ways to Handle the Challenges
of the Classroom Effectively
Annette L. Breaux and Elizabeth Breaux

This book is ideal for high-interest staff development workshops or new teacher induction programs. It helps new teachers—and experienced ones—find solutions to common classroom challenges. It presents 25 real scenarios along with "What's Effective," "What's NOT Effective," and "Bottom Line" strategies for handling the most common teacher challenges.

This book shows teachers how to:

- get students to do what you want them to do.
- deal with disrespectful student behaviors and handle "I don't care" attitudes.
- deal with parents and difficult coworkers.
- solve other common teaching challenges.

REAL Teachers, REAL Challenges, REAL Solutions: 25 Ways to Handle the Challenges of the Classroom Effectively is for:

- new teachers who need common-sense answers to common teaching challenges.
- experienced teachers who seek to become even more effective.

2003, 120 pp. paperback1-930556-64-0
$24.95 plus shipping and handling

Order form on page 143

101 "Answers" for New Teachers & Their Mentors:
Effective Teaching Tips for Daily Classroom Use
Annette L. and Elizabeth Breaux

"There is no one I recommend more highly than Annette Breaux."

Harry K. Wong, author
The First Days of School

101 "Answers" for New Teachers & Their Mentors: Effective Teaching Tips for Daily Classroom Use generates instant impact on teaching and learning. Organized so new teachers can read it by themselves, it can also be studied collaboratively with veteran teachers who have been selected to mentor them.

This book—

♦ offers common sense strategies for any teacher seeking to be more effective.

♦ supports and sustains master classroom teachers who need help mastering their roles as mentors.

♦ stimulates and organizes interactive sessions between new teachers and their mentors.

Contents

♦ Classroom Management

♦ Planning

♦ Instruction

♦ Professionalism, Attitudes, and Behaviors of Effective Teachers

♦ Motivation and Rapport

♦ A Teacher's Influence

2003, 180 pp. paperback 1-930556-48-9
$29.95 plus shipping and handling

Order form on page 143

Interested in ordering multiple copies of Eye On Education titles?

- ♦ Order copies as "welcome" gifts for all of your *new* teachers.
- ♦ Order copies as holiday gifts for *all* of your teachers.
- ♦ Assign them as required reading in new teacher induction programs.
- ♦ Assign them in book study groups with experienced teachers.

Our discount schedule:

			Discount*
10 – 24	copies	=	5%
25 – 74	copies	=	10%
75 – 99	copies	=	15%
100 +	copies	=	20%

(plus shipping and handling.
Feel free to call for more information)

*Note: These discounts apply to orders of individual titles and do not apply to combinations of more than one title.

6 Depot Way West
Larchmont, NY 10538
Phone (914) 833–0551
Fax (914) 833–0761
www.eyeoneducation.com

ORDER FORM

☐ **What Great Teachers Do** *Differently*: **14 Things That Matter Most.** Whitaker. 2003. 130 pp. paperback 1-930556-69-1. $29.95 plus shipping and handling

☐ **What Great Principals Do** *Differently*: **15 Things That Matter Most.** Whitaker. 2002. 130 pp. paperback 1-930556-47-0. $29.95 plus shipping and handling.

☐ **Dealing with Difficult Teachers,** Second Edition. Whitaker. 2002. 208 pp. paperback 1-930556-45-4. $29.95 plus shipping and handling.

☐ **Motivating and Inspiring Teachers: The Educator's Guide for Building Staff Morale.** Whitaker, Whitaker, and Lumpa. 2000. 252 pp. paperback 1-883001-99-4. $34.95 plus shipping and handling.

☐ **Teaching Matters: Motivating & Inspiring Yourself.** Whitaker and Whitaker. 2002. 150 pp. paperback. 1-930556-35-7. $24.95 plus shipping and handling.

☐ **Feeling Great! The Educator's Guide for Eating Better, Exercising Smarter, and Feeling Your Best.** Whitaker and Winkle. 2002. 150 pp. paperback 1-930556-38-1. $24.95 plus shipping and handling.

☐ **Dealing with Difficult Parents (And with Parents in Difficult Situations).** Whitaker and Fiore. 2001. 175 pp. paperback 1-930556-09-8. $29.95 plus shipping and handling.

☐ **REAL Teachers, REAL Challenges, REAL Solutions: 25 Ways to Handle the Challenges of the Classroom Effectively.** Breaux and Breaux. 2003. 120 pp. paperback 1-930556-64-0. $24.95 plus shipping and handling.

☐ **101 "Answers" for New Teachers and Their Mentors: Effective Teaching Tips for Daily Classroom Use.** Breaux. 2003. 176 pp. paperback 1-930556-48-9. $29.95 plus shipping and handling.

Fill in your address on other side

Please place your check and/or purchase order with this form in an envelope and mail to *Eye On Education*. If you are not satisfied with any book, simply return it within 30 days in saleable condition for full credit or refund.

Ship to: _____
         Name

_____
School

_____
Address

_____
City   State   Zip

_____
Phone   Your title

Bill to: _____
        Name

_____
School

_____
Address

_____
City   State   Zip

_____
Phone   Your title

Subtotal (books)   _____

Shipping and Handling   _____

Total   _____

Shipping and Handling:

1 Book—Add $6.00   2 Books—Add $10.00   3 Books—Add $13.00

4 Books—Add $15.00   5–7 Books—Add $17.00   8–11 Books—Add $19.00

Method of Payment (choose one):
☐ Check (enclosed)   ☐ Credit Card   ☐ Purchase Order

_____   _____

Credit card # (Visa, Master Card, Discover) or PO #   Expiration Date

6 Depot Way West
Larchmont, N.Y. 10538
(914) 833–0551 Phone (914) 833–0761 Fax
www.eyeoneducation.com